# PLAYWAY *plus*

Günter Gerngross · Herbert Puchta · Carmen Becker

## FIT IN ENGLISCH

# 1 Numbers and colours

**1** **Write the words.**

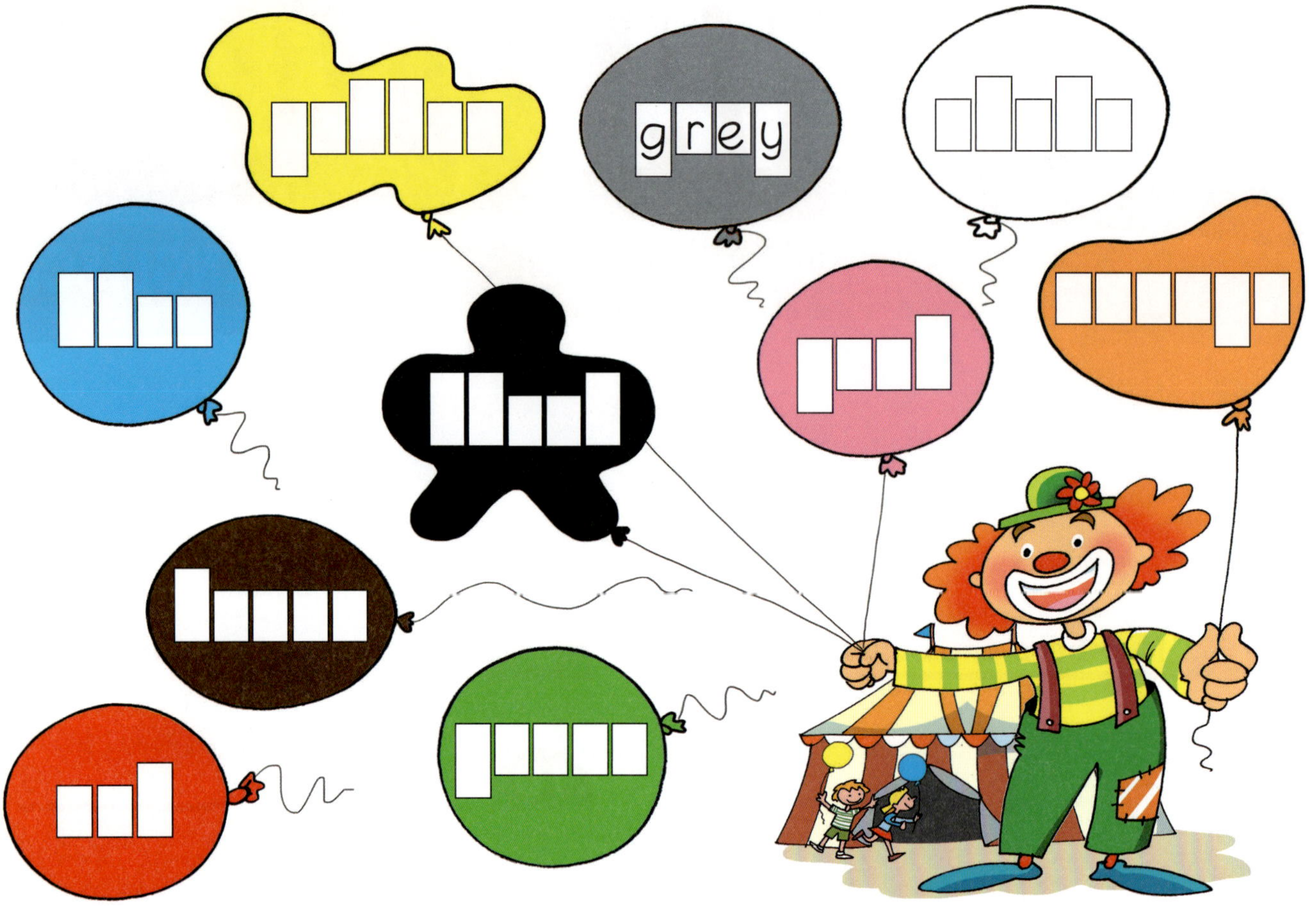

grey

**2** **Look and write.**

| | | |
|---|---|---|
| eleven | twenty-three | nineteen | twenty-four | thirteen |
| twenty-five | twelve | ten | fifteen |

_____     _____     _____

_____     _____     _____

_____     _____     _____

PLAYWAY plus • G. Gerngross, H. Puchta, C. Becker • © 2012 HELBLING, Rum/Innsbruck

Hinweis:
*is* verwendest du für eine Person ⚊
*are* verwendest du für mehrere Personen ⚊⚊

**3** How old are they? Complete the sentences.

1

Bob is ___*eleven*___ .

2

Molly and Kate are _____ .

3

Olivia is _____ .

4

John and Sarah _____ .

5

Chris _____ .

6

Nicky _____ .

**4** Write.

1 twelve + ✖ = twenty-eight

2 twenty-three − ☺ = eighteen

3 ten + eleven = ★

4 four + ✖ = _____

5 thirty − ★ = _____

6 ☺ + forty-one = _____

7 ✖ + sixty-two = _____

8 ★ + ✖ = _____

9 ✖ + ☺ = _____

✖ = _____
☺ = _____
★ = _____

**5** **Look and write.**

My name is Jason.
I'm nine.
My favourite colour is blue.

Jason / 9 / blue

My name is _____

I'm _____

My favourite colour is _____

Kelly / 6 / green

Pete / 11 / yellow

_____

_____

_____

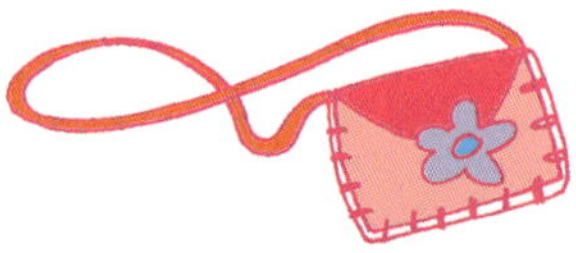

Karen / 14 / pink

_____

_____

13

_____

_____

Will / 13 / orange

PLAYWAY plus • G. Gerngross, H. Puchta, C. Becker • © 2012 HELBLING, Rum/Innsbruck

**6** **Look, count and write the numbers. Then complete the dialogue.**

| | | | | | |
|---|---|---|---|---|---|
| _9_ | ___ | ___ | ___ | ___ | ___ |

How many planes are there? – Nine.

How many _____ are there? – Two.

How many boats _____ ? – _____ .

_____ skateboards are there? – _____ .

_____ are there? – Seven.

_____ balls _____ ? – _____ .

Now stick the flower on your English Certificate!

**1** Find and circle the ten words. ↓ →

| Z | K | O | E | C | D | K | M | N | S |
|---|---|---|---|---|---|---|---|---|---|
| G | R | U | B | B | E | R | W | S | W |
| E | B | O | O | K | Y | Y | M | C | B |
| Z | I | W | J | O | W | C | G | H | O |
| F | R | U | L | E | R | P | I | O | A |
| S | U | V | I | P | E | N | M | O | R |
| D | P | E | N | C | I | L | G | L | D |
| E | Q | W | Y | G | J | T | G | B | Q |
| S | I | T | F | L | K | M | P | A | Q |
| K | W | N | F | D | O | O | R | G | E |
| F | M | S | C | I | S | S | O | R | S |
| A | C | L | P | L | I | W | C | B | G |

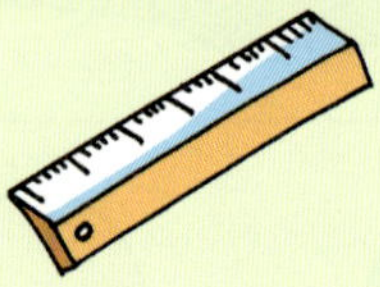

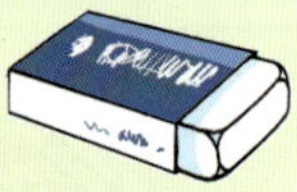

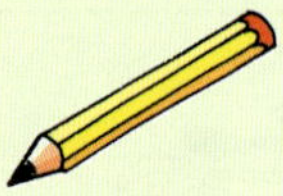

**2** Write the words.

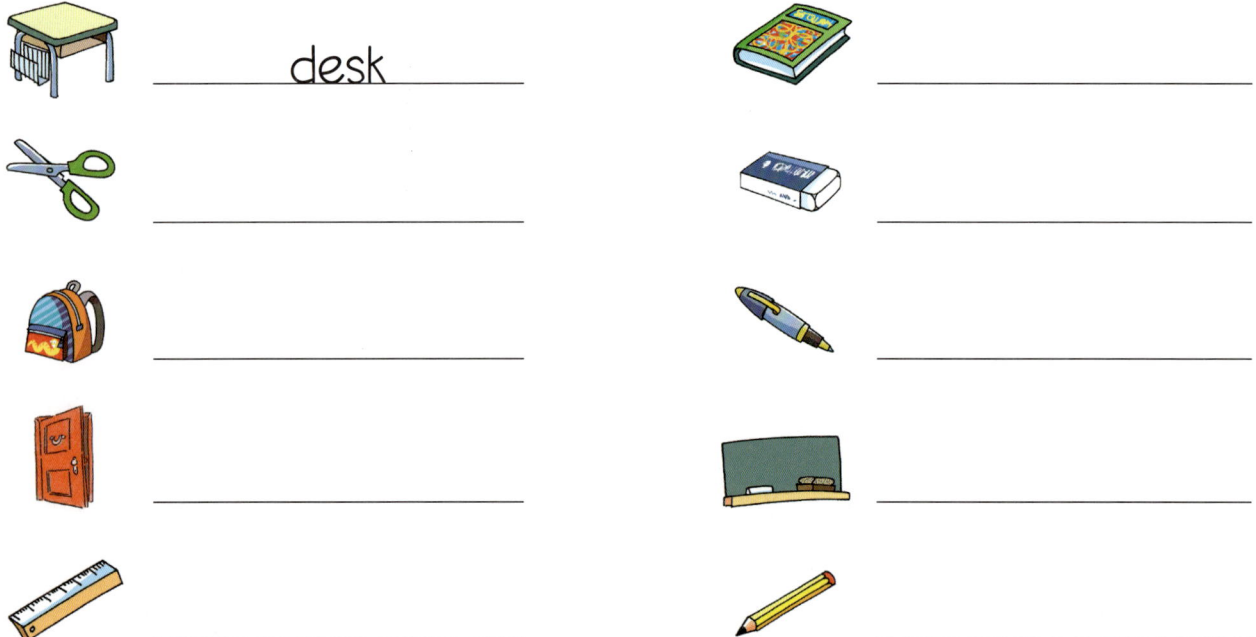

desk

PLAYWAY plus • G. Gerngross, H. Puchta, C. Becker • © 2012 HELBLING, Rum/Innsbruck

**3**  **Match. Write the numbers.**

1  Who's your English teacher?

2  Let's sing a song.

3  How many children are in your class?

4  How are you?

◯ Twenty-two.

◯ It's Ms Clark.

◯ I'm fine. Thank you.

◯ No, let's play a game.

Hinweis:
*Who's* your best friend?
= *Who is* your best friend?

**4**  **Look and fill in the missing words. Then write about Linda's desk.**

On Benny's desk there is a

_pen_____ ,

there are two _____ ,

there are three _____

and there are five

_____ .

Hinweis:
*there is* verwendest du für die *Einzahl*
*there are* verwendest du für die *Mehrzahl*

On Linda's desk there is a

_____

_____

_____

_____

_____

_____ .

**5**   **Write the sentences.**

## She is … / He is …

> taking his bag          checking her watch        having a glass of milk
> putting books in her bag     walking to school         reading a book

She is _____ .

He is _____ .

_____ .

_____ .

_____ .

_____ .

PLAYWAY plus • G. Gerngross, H. Puchta, C. Becker • © 2012 HELBLING, Rum/Innsbruck

**6** **Read and fill in the missing words.**

| friend | play | children | walk | eleven | home | at nine |

Dear Hannah,

I like my new school here in London. There are twenty-six

_____ in my class. Our teacher is

Mrs Black. I like her. My best _____

is Mohammed. He is _____ .

We often _____ football in the park.

School starts _____ o'clock, not at eight.

I can _____ to school. I come _____

at half past three. Please write soon.

Peter

**7** **Read the text in 6 and write the answers.**

Hinweis:
What's = What is

Where is Peter's school? _____

How many children are in Peter's class? _____

What's his teacher's name? _____

What's his best friend's name? _____

How old is his friend? _____

When does school start? _____

Now stick the flower on your English Certificate!

**1** Write the words.

| | | |
|---|---|---|
| ugebid | ~~ehspe~~ | ibatrb |
| ebe | cudk | ogd |
| oinl | rfgo | act |
| eoshr | okmeyn | nseak |

**1**

sheep

**2**

_____

**3**

_____

**4**

_____

**5**

_____

**6**

_____

**7**

_____

**8**

_____

**9**

_____

**10**

_____

**11**

_____

**12**

_____

PLAYWAY plus • G. Gerngross, H. Puchta, C. Becker • © 2012 HELBLING, Rum/Innsbruck

**2** **Read and write.**

> He has got a dog.    They have got a dog.    I have got a dog.    She has got a dog.

I have got a dog.

_____

_____

_____

**3** **Look and write sentences.**

She _____

_____

_____

_____

**4** **Look at the animals. Read and complete the sentences.**

1. It can run fast. It eats grass. It likes carrots. It can't fly.

   It's a _____ .

2. It can fly. It can swim. It lays eggs.

   It's a _____ .

3. It eats other animals. It can't fly. It can run fast.

   It's a _____ .

4. It lays eggs. It can swim. It eats flies. It can't fly.

   It's a _____ .

5. It lays eggs. It can't fly. It eats other animals.

   It's a _____ .

6. It lays eggs. It can fly. It can't swim.

   It's a _____ .

**5** **Look at the animals and write three sentences from 4.**

1

2

Hinweis:
Verwende die Sätze in Übung 4 als Hilfe.

_____ It can't fly. _____

_____

_____

_____

_____

_____

PLAYWAY plus • G. Gerngross, H. Puchta, C. Becker • © 2012 HELBLING, Rum/Innsbruck

**6**  **Who is it? Look, read and write the names.**

Lucy      Jane      Anne

① She has got a pony. It's black and white. It's seven years old. _____

② She has got a pony. It's black, brown and white. It's four years old. _____

③ She has got a pony. It's black and white. It's three years old. _____

**7**  **Look and write. Use _he, she_ and _they._**

Hannah

① She has got _____

It's _____

It's _____

_____

**Hinweis:**
he/she **has** got
they **have** got

Liz and Mike

② _____

_____

_____

_____

Allan

③ _____

_____

_____

_____

Now stick the flower on your English Certificate!

## 1 Circle the words. Then write.

(hair)kneenosemoutheyehandeararmlegfootteethtoesheadshoulderfingers

hair

PLAYWAY plus • G. Gerngross, H. Puchta, C. Becker • © 2012 HELBLING, Rum/Innsbruck

**2   Read, look and write.**

| Touch your nose. | Shake your arms. | Touch your knee. |
| Clap your hands. | Touch your ear. | Shake your head. |

1.

_____

2.

_____

3.

_____

4.

_____

5.

_____

6.

_____

**3   What's missing? Write.**

Hinweis: her hair   his hair

 _____ her hair _____

 _____

 _____

 _____

 _____

 _____

 _____

 _____

**4** Read the two dialogues. Look at the pictures and fill in the correct number.

> (1) *Dad:* Have some breakfast, Philip.
> *Philip:* No, thanks, Dad. I feel sick.
> *Dad:* Oh, I'm sorry.
>   Would you like a cup of tea?
> *Philip:* Yes, please, Dad.

> (2) *James:* Ouch!
> *Dad:* What's the matter, James?
> *James:* My right arm hurts.

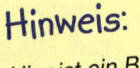

Hinweis:
Hier ist ein Bild zu viel!

**5** Fill in the numbers. Then write.

1

○ *Emma:* I feel sick.

○ *Mum:* Yes, Emma. What's the matter?

(1) *Emma:* Mum?

○ *Emma:* Thanks, Mum.

○ *Mum:* Have a cup of tea.

Mum? _____

_____

_____

_____

_____

2

○ *Sofia:* Ouch. Don't touch it.

○ *Mum:* Let me see.

(1) *Sofia:* Ouch!

○ *Mum:* What's the problem?

○ *Mum:* I'm sorry.

○ *Sofia:* My shoulder hurts.

Ouch! _____

_____

_____

_____

_____

PLAYWAY plus • G. Gerngross, H. Puchta, C. Becker • © 2012 HELBLING, Rum/Innsbruck

## 6 Read and colour.

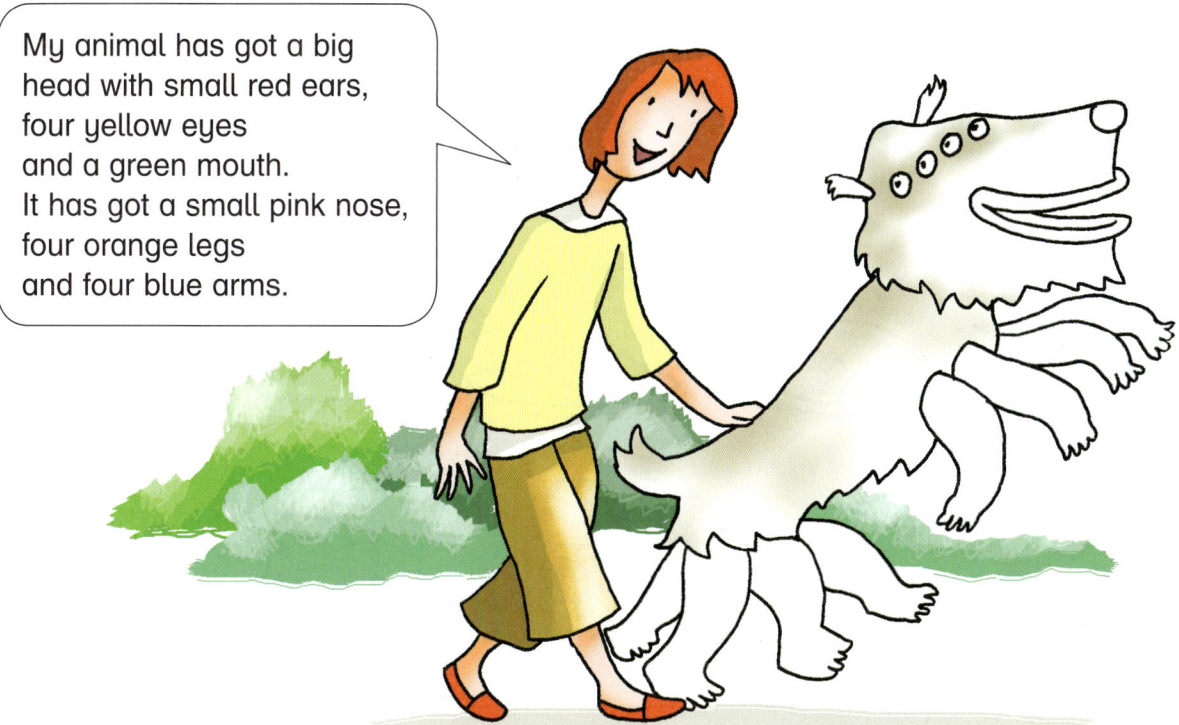

My animal has got a big
head with small red ears,
four yellow eyes
and a green mouth.
It has got a small pink nose,
four orange legs
and four blue arms.

## 7 Look and write.

**Hinweis:**
Verwende den Text in Übung **6** als Hilfe.

*My animal has got* __________

____________________

____________________

____________________

____________________

____________________

____________________

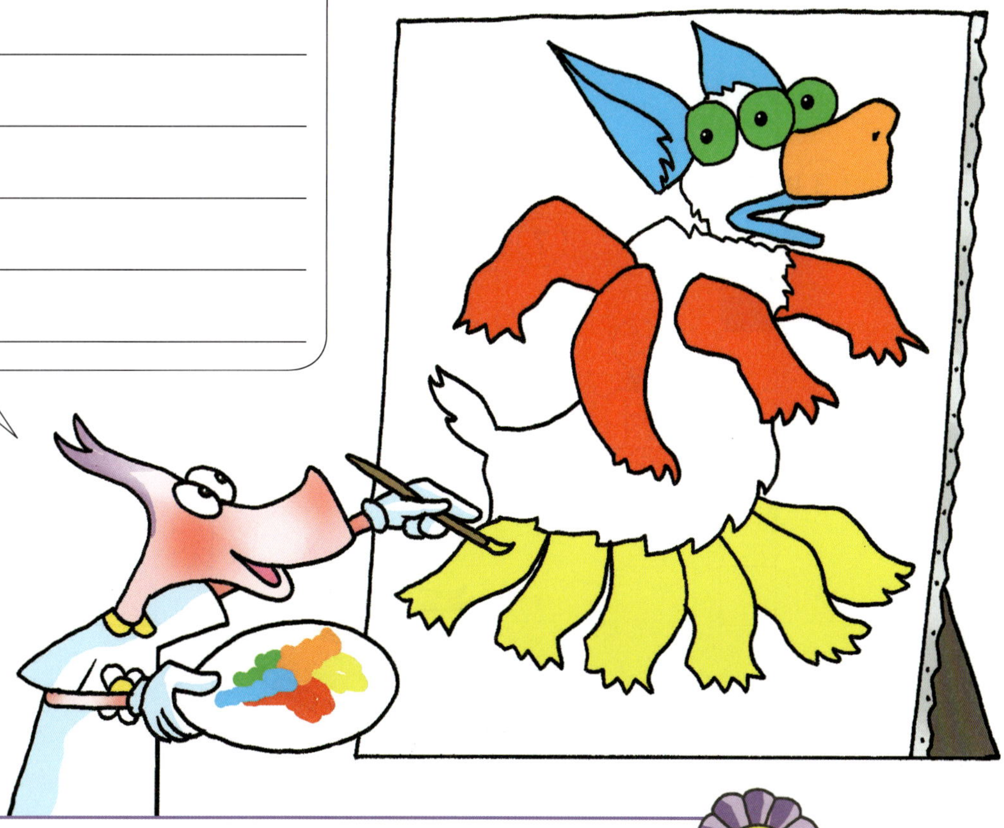

Now stick the flower on your English Certificate!

**1** Do the crossword.

PLAYWAY plus • G. Gerngross, H. Puchta, C. Becker • © 2012 HELBLING, Rum/Innsbruck

**2** **Match. Write the numbers.**

1 Do you like spinach?

2 What have you got?

3 Can I have a sandwich, please?

4 I'm very hungry.

○ Here you are.

○ Yes, I do.

○ So am I.

○ Two bananas and two sandwiches.

**3** **Read and draw**   **or** .

1 **Mark:** I like pizza. I don't like fish. My favourite food is chicken.

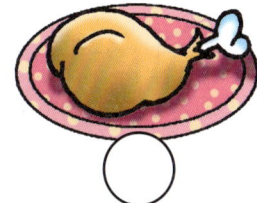  

2 **Katie:** I like cake. I don't like cheese. My favourite food is ham.

3 **Toby:** I like fish. I don't like pizza. My favourite food is spaghetti.

4 **Eve:** I like bananas. I don't like apples. My favourite fruit is strawberries.

**4**  **Look at the pictures. Write the names.**

I like pizza. I don't like spaghetti.

_____

Sue

Tom

I like fish. I don't like cake.

_____

I like chips. I don't like spinach.

_____

Ann

Emma

I like apples. I don't like pizza.

_____

**5**  **Look and write.**

I like _____

_____

_____

_____

_____

PLAYWAY plus • G. Gerngross, H. Puchta, C. Becker • © 2012 HELBLING, Rum/Innsbruck

**6** **Look and write the sentences.**

> They like apples.     She likes chicken and chips.
> He likes sandwiches.     She doesn't like spinach.
> He doesn't like peas.     They don't like sausages.

**Hinweis:**

he/she *likes* | he/she *doesn't like*
they *like* | they *don't like*

1

2

3

_____

_____

4

5

6

_____

_____

**7** **Look and write.**

1

2

3

_____

_____

Now stick the flower on your English Certificate!

**1** **Circle the words. Then write.**

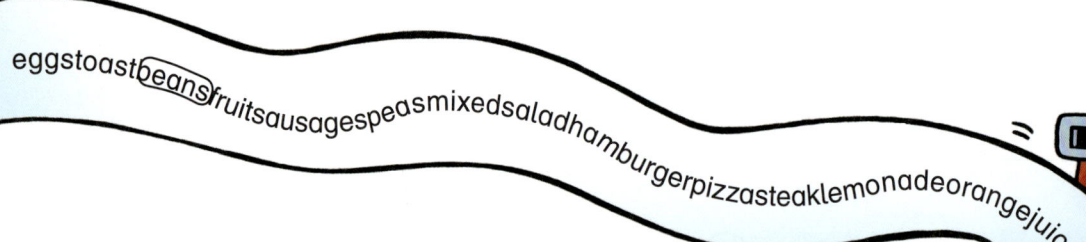

eggstoast(beans)fruitsausagespeasmixedsaladhamburgerpizzasteaklemonadeorangejuice

## Menu

beans

_____

_____

_____

_____

_____

_____

_____

_____

_____

_____

_____

PLAYWAY plus • G. Gerngross, H. Puchta, C. Becker • © 2012 HELBLING, Rum/Innsbruck

**2** Look and write *Linda*, *Benny*, *Mum* or *Dad*.

I'm having steak, peas and orange juice.

I'm having a hamburger, a mixed salad and cola.

I'm having sausages, peas and lemonade.

I'm having a mixed salad, pizza and mineral water.

_____     _____     _____     _____

**3** Read. Then complete the sentences.

|         | hamburgers | fish and chips | pizza | sausages | mixed salad |
|---------|:----------:|:--------------:|:-----:|:--------:|:-----------:|
| Noah    | ☺          | ☹              | ☺     | ☺        | ☹           |
| Kirsten | ☹          | ☺              | ☺     | ☹        | ☺           |

① Noah likes hamburgers. He doesn't like fish and chips.
He _____

_____

_____

② Kirsten doesn't like hamburgers. She likes fish and chips.

_____

_____

_____

**4** **Read and complete the dialogues.**

| orange juice | pizza | mineral water | thank you | chips |
|---|---|---|---|---|
| Here | Would | steak | drink | ~~eat~~ |

What would you like to _____ eat _____ ?

I'd like 🍝 _____
and _____ , please.

Hinweis:
*I'd* like = I *would* like
*we'd* like = we *would* like

What would you like to
_____ ?

I'd like a 🍕 _____ , please.

We'd like 🍾 _____ and
an 🥤 _____ , please.

_____ you are.

_____
you like a dessert?

Thank you.

No, _____ .

PLAYWAY plus • G. Gerngross, H. Puchta, C. Becker • © 2012 HELBLING, Rum/Innsbruck

**5** Fill in the numbers. Then write the dialogue.

( ) An orange juice, please.

( ) I'd like a pizza and a mixed salad.

(6) Yes, I'd like a fruit salad, please.

( ) And what would you like to drink?

( ) Would you like a dessert?

(1) What would you like to eat?

What would you like to eat?

_____

_____

_____

_____

_____

_____

**6** Look and write.

**Hinweis:**
Verwende den Text in Übung **5** als Hilfe.

What would you like to eat?

_____ a s_____ with

p_____ and b_____ , please.

I'd like c_____ and r_____ , please.

And _____ to drink?

A c_____ , please .

A l_____ , please.

Would you like a dessert?

Yes, I'd like a f_____ s_____ , please .

An i_____ , please.

Now stick the flower on your English Certificate!

**1** **Write the words.**

> grandpa     sister     grandma     mum     ~~brother~~
>
> brother    grandma     dad     grandpa     sister

DANIEL

This is me.

AMY

MIA

JEFF

TOM

_brother_

JULIA

MARK

CONNOR

SUSAN

LIZ

FRANK

**2** **Read and write.**

Who is Daniel's mum? _____ .

Who is Mark's dad? _____ .

Who are Tom's sisters? _____ .

Who is Julia's mum? _____ .

Who is Mia's dad? _____ .

Julia is Amy's _____ .

Jeff and Tom are Daniel's _____ .

Frank is Mia's _____ .

Connor is Julia's _____ .

Liz is Jeff's _____ .

PLAYWAY plus • G. Gerngross, H. Puchta, C. Becker • © 2012 HELBLING, Rum/Innsbruck

**3** **Read and fill in the numbers.**

Hinweis:
there's = there is

**1**
Hi, my name is Leah.
In my family there's my mum,
my two brothers, my sister
Patricia and me.

**2**
Hi, I'm Holly.
In my family there's my brother
Christopher, my grandpa,
my mum and me.

**3**
Hi, I'm Jessica.
In my family there's my dad,
my mum, my grandpa,
my grandma and me.

**4**
Hi, I'm Grace. In my family
there's my grandma Rose,
my grandma Eileen, my dad,
my mum, my sister and me.

**4** **Write the words.**

| pyaph | das | ridet | yagnr | draces |

    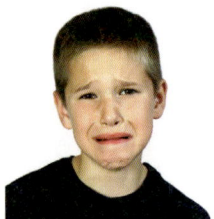

_____ _____ _____ _____ _____

**5** **Read the story. Look at the pictures and fill in the numbers.**

1
Dad:      Are you sad, Simon?
Simon:   No, I'm scared.
Dad:      What's the problem?

2
Simon:   There's a dog in our garden.
Dad:      A dog?
Simon:   Yes.

3
Dad:      OK, I'll go and check.
*Dad goes out …*

4
*… and comes back very fast.*
Simon:   Dad, are you scared too?
Dad:      Yes, I'm scared.

5
Dad:      The dog is very big and angry.

PLAYWAY plus • G. Gerngross, H. Puchta, C. Becker • © 2012 HELBLING, Rum/Innsbruck

**6**  **Fill in the numbers. Then write the dialogue.**

◯  What's the problem?

◯  Would you like some bread with ham?

①  Are you angry?

◯  Yes, please.

◯  No, I'm not.

◯  I'm hungry.

?

Are you angry?
_____
_____
_____
_____
_____
_____

**7**  **Read and complete the sentences.**

| nine | he | she | her | his | is | got |

My name _____ Gabriel. I'm _____ .

I've _____ a brother and a sister.

_____ name is John and _____ name is Jennifer.

_____ is six and _____ is three.

Hinweis:
Wörter am Satzanfang werden mit großen Anfangsbuchstaben geschrieben.

**8**  **Look and write.**

My name is Kate. I'm _____
_____
_____
_____
_____
_____
_____

Kate 10

Sarah
7

5
Rick

Hinweis:
Verwende den Text in Übung 7 als Hilfe.

Now stick the flower on your English Certificate!

**1**   **Write.**

| window     table     chair     wardrobe     lamp     stairs     bed     sofa |

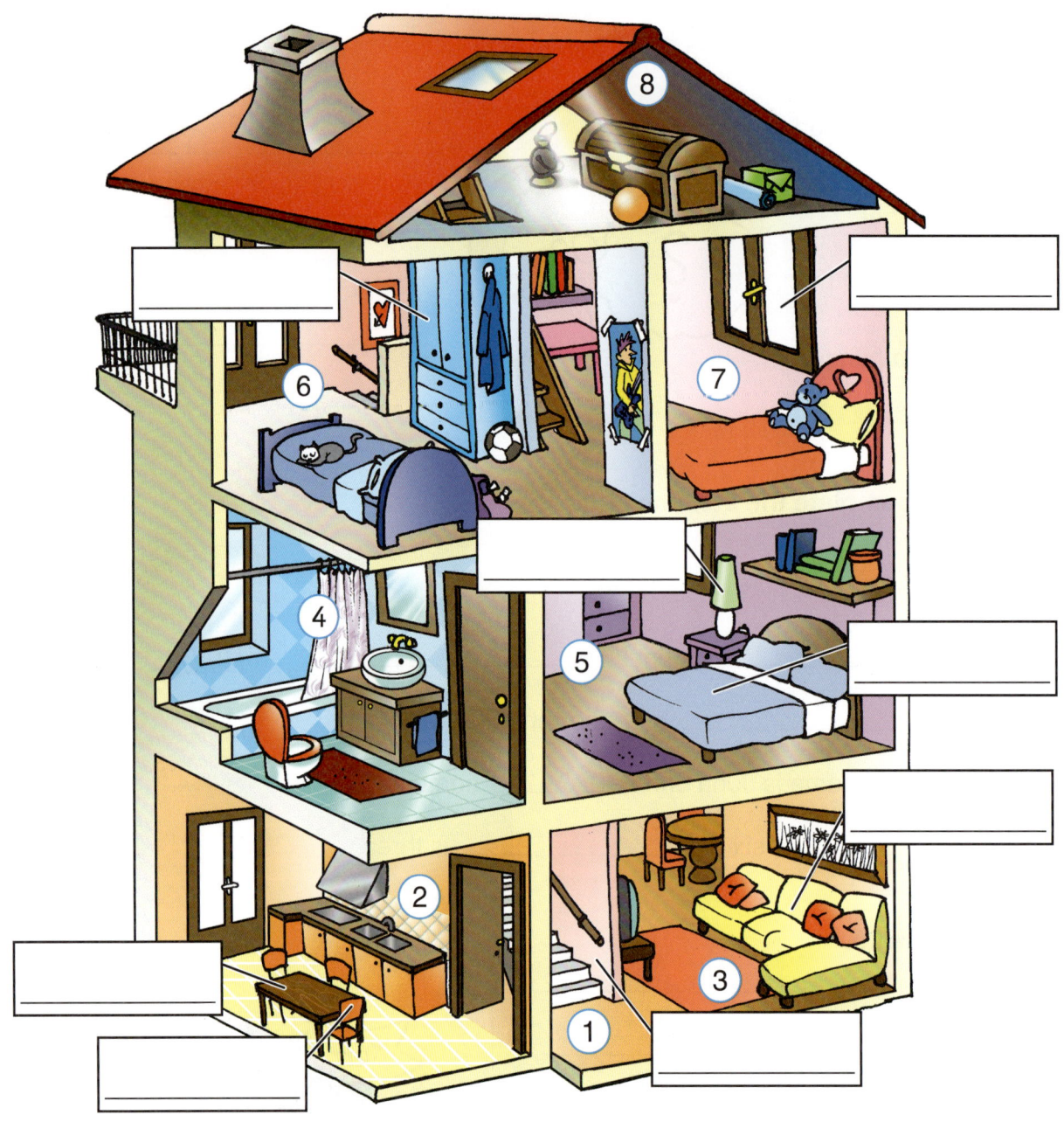

**2**   **Look at the numbers in 1. Write the names of the rooms.**

| George's room     ~~hall~~     Lydia's room     living room |
| bathroom     bedroom     attic     kitchen |

1   hall        5   _____

2   _____     6   _____

3   _____     7   _____

4   _____     8   _____

PLAYWAY plus • G. Gerngross, H. Puchta, C. Becker • © 2012 HELBLING, Rum/Innsbruck

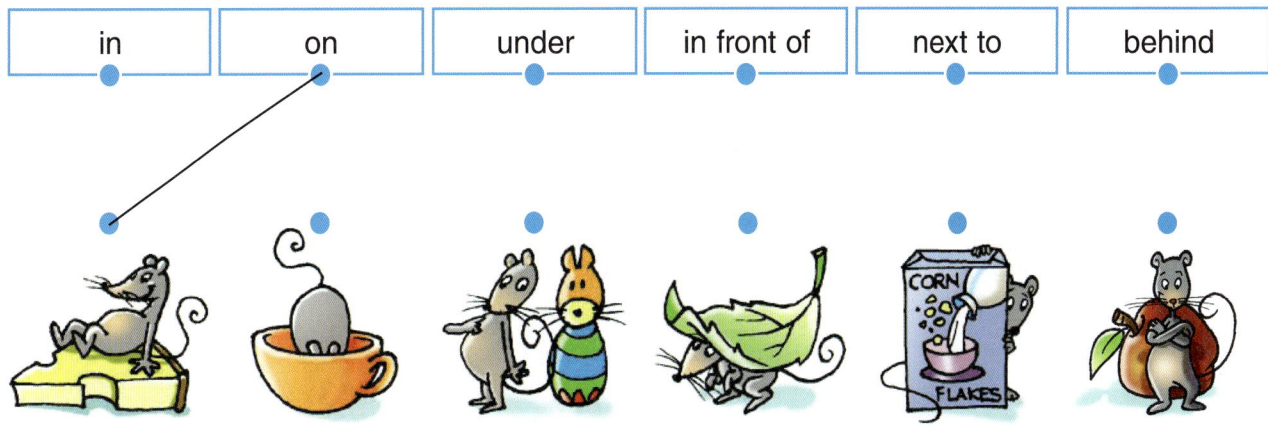

**3  Look and match.**

| in | on | under | in front of | next to | behind |
|---|---|---|---|---|---|

**4  Look and write.**

1. There are jeans _____under_____ the bed.
2. There is a plane _____ the wardrobe.
3. There _____ two chairs _____ the sofa.
4. There _____ a ball _____ the bed.
5. There _____ a lamp _____ the sofa.
6. There _____ two books _____ the green chair.
7. There _____ a pen _____ the brown chair.
8. There _____ a small table _____ the sofa.
9. There _____ an umbrella _____ the schoolbag.

Hinweis:
*there is* verwendest du für die Einzahl
*there are* verwendest du für die Mehrzahl

**5** **Read and fill in the missing words.**

| is | interesting | favourite | big | things |
|---|---|---|---|---|

LONDON EYE

Hi Anna,

London is great. There are lots of _____ to do.

My _____ place is the London Eye.

From up there you can see how _____ London is.

There is also a great museum, the Natural History Museum.

There _____ a big fossil of the

Brontosaurus and many other _____ things.

Love,
Ella

**6** **Write the sentences.**

| Take off your shoes, please. | Where's the bathroom, please? |
|---|---|
| What are you doing in the kitchen? | Let's go to the attic. |

PLAYWAY plus • G. Gerngross, H. Puchta, C. Becker • © 2012 HELBLING, Rum/Innsbruck

**Liebe Eltern!**
**Liebe Lehrkräfte!**

PLAYWAY plus bereitet die Kinder in nachhaltiger Weise auf den Englischunterricht an den weiterführenden Schulen vor und erleichtert ihnen damit den Übergang. Mit Hilfe vielfältiger Übungen wiederholen die Kinder den in der Grundschule vermittelten Wortschatz, der im ersten Jahr der weiterführenden Schule vertieft und erweitert wird. Dieses Wiederholen von Wortschatz und Strukturen ist entscheidend für das Abspeichern im Langzeitgedächtnis.
Darüber hinaus trainieren die Übungen das Lesen und Schreiben der englischen Sprache.
Beim Schreiben der Wörter wird den Kindern meist Hilfestellung angeboten. Dadurch lernen und wiederholen sie die englische Rechtschreibung von wichtigen Wörtern.

PLAYWAY plus beinhaltet 14 Themen auf jeweils vier Seiten, die unabhängig voneinander bearbeitet werden können.
Die Übungen zu jedem Thema sind nach folgendem Schema aufgebaut:

- Die Übungen der ersten Seite wiederholen und festigen den Wortschatz.
- Auf der zweiten Seite wird dieser Wortschatz in einen Zusammenhang eingebettet.
- Auf den Seiten drei und vier bearbeiten die Kinder kleine Texte mit Hilfe von Bildern oder anderen Hilfestellungen.

Aufgrund dieses Schemas ist es ratsam, dass alle Aufgaben zu einem Thema der Reihe nach bearbeitet werden.
Es empfiehlt sich, dass die Lösungen mit Bleistift eingetragen werden – so können etwaige Fehler leichter korrigiert werden. Wenn die Übungen auf einer Seite ausgefüllt sind, sehen die Kinder im Lösungsheft nach, ob alles richtig ist. Wurden Fehler gemacht, ist es sinnvoll, die Eintragungen auszuradieren und die Übung nach einiger Zeit nochmals zu bearbeiten.

**Hinweis:**
*Immer wieder finden sich im Buch Notizzettel mit Hinweisen, die bei besonders schwierigen Aufgaben helfen.*

Im Anhang des Buches befindet sich eine alphabetische Wortliste (Englisch – Deutsch / Deutsch – Englisch), sowie eine Übersicht zu den Zahlen, Fragewörtern und Fürwörtern, damit die Kinder – sollten sie ein Wort nicht wissen – selbst nachschlagen können.

Sind alle Seiten zu einem Thema erfolgreich absolviert, belohnen sich die Kinder, indem sie den dazugehörigen Blumensticker aus der Heftmitte nehmen und ihn im „English Certificate" ganz hinten im Heft auf die Blume mit dem Namen des Themas kleben. Hat das Kind alle Themen abgeschlossen, ergibt sich dadurch ein Gesamtbild von Max mit einem Blumenstrauß.

**Tipps zur optimalen Förderung der Kinder:**
- Wichtig ist, dass die Kinder regelmäßig und in kleinen Schritten arbeiten.
- Loben Sie die Kinder, wenn sie ein Thema bearbeitet haben.
- Lassen Sie die Kinder möglichst selbstständig arbeiten. Die Arbeitsanweisungen sind leicht verständlich; sollten die Kinder dennoch damit Probleme haben, erklären Sie ihnen die Aufgabenstellung auf Deutsch.
- Fördern Sie die Motivation der Kinder, indem Sie sie loben, wenn sie den Sticker in das „English Certificate" am Ende des Heftes eingeklebt haben.

PLAYWAY plus – LÖSUNGSHEFT • G. Gerngross, H. Puchta, C. Becker • © 2012 HELBLING, Rum/Innsbruck

## 1 Numbers and colours

**1 Write the words.**

yellow, grey, white, blue, orange, black, pink, brown, green, red

**2 Look and write.**

eleven   twenty-three   nineteen   twenty-four   thirteen
twenty-five   twelve   ten   fifteen

| 15 | 24 | 11 |
|---|---|---|
| fifteen | twenty-four | eleven |
| 23 | 12 | 25 |
| twenty-three | twelve | twenty-five |
| 10 | 19 | 13 |
| ten | nineteen | thirteen |

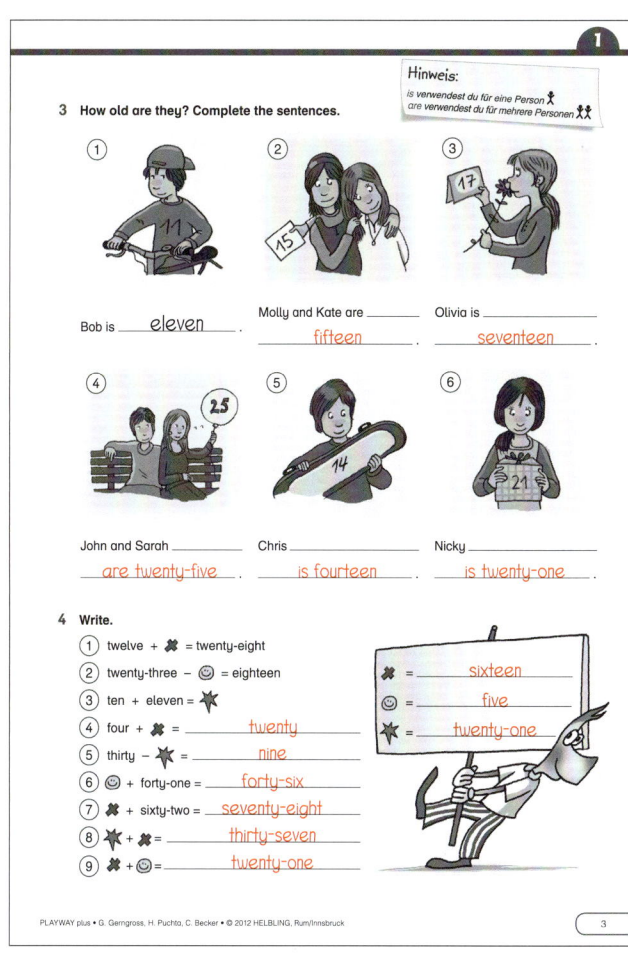

**3 How old are they? Complete the sentences.**

Hinweis:
is verwendest du für eine Person
are verwendest du für mehrere Personen

① Bob is __eleven__ .

② Molly and Kate are ____ . fifteen .

③ Olivia is ____ . seventeen .

④ John and Sarah ____ . are twenty-five .

⑤ Chris ____ . is fourteen .

⑥ Nicky ____ . is twenty-one .

**4 Write.**

① twelve + ✱ = twenty-eight
② twenty-three – ☺ = eighteen
③ ten + eleven = ★
④ four + ✱ = __twenty__
⑤ thirty – ★ = __nine__
⑥ ☺ + forty-one = __forty-six__
⑦ ✱ + sixty-two = __seventy-eight__
⑧ ★ + ✱ = __thirty-seven__
⑨ ✱ + ☺ = __twenty-one__

✱ = sixteen
☺ = five
★ = twenty-one

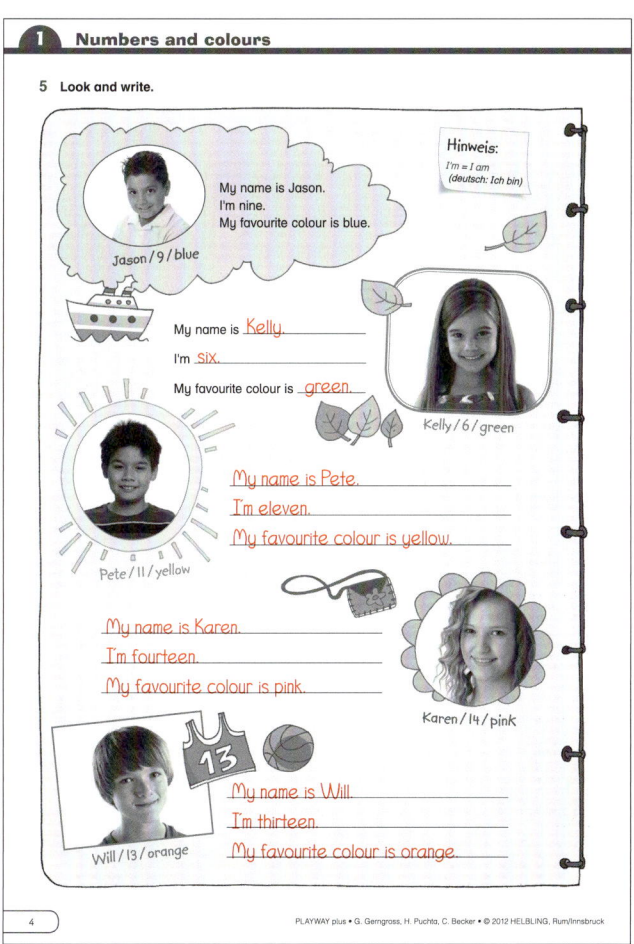

## 1 Numbers and colours

**5 Look and write.**

My name is Jason.
I'm nine.
My favourite colour is blue.

Jason / 9 / blue

Hinweis:
I'm = I am
(deutsch: Ich bin)

My name is Kelly.
I'm six.
My favourite colour is green.

Kelly / 6 / green

My name is Pete.
I'm eleven.
My favourite colour is yellow.

Pete / 11 / yellow

My name is Karen.
I'm fourteen.
My favourite colour is pink.

Karen / 14 / pink

My name is Will.
I'm thirteen.
My favourite colour is orange.

Will / 13 / orange

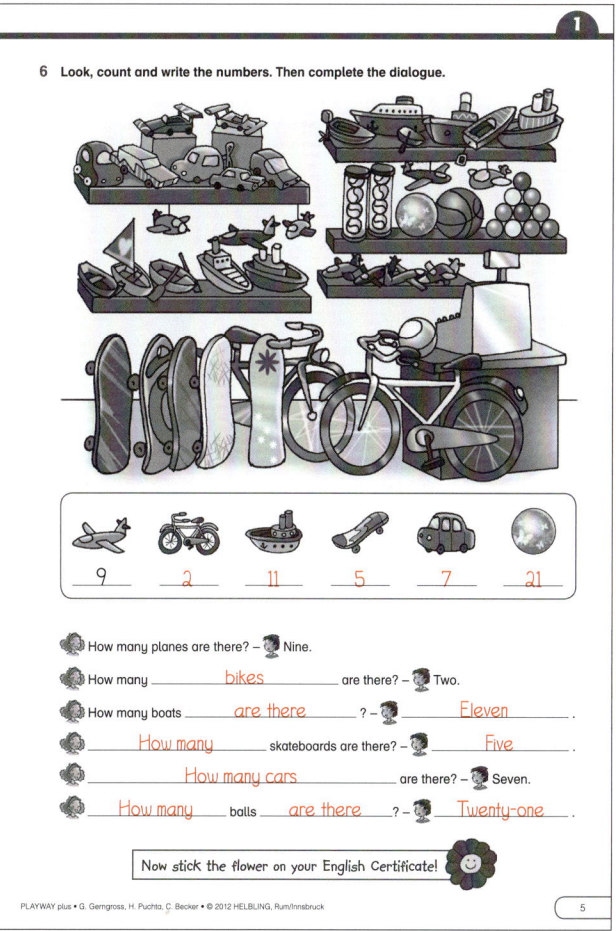

**6 Look, count and write the numbers. Then complete the dialogue.**

| ✈ | 🚲 | ⛵ | 🛹 | 🚗 | ⚽ |
|---|---|---|---|---|---|
| 9 | 2 | 11 | 5 | 7 | 21 |

How many planes are there? – Nine.
How many __bikes__ are there? – Two.
How many boats __are there__ ? – __Eleven__
__How many__ skateboards are there? – __Five__
__How many cars__ are there? – Seven.
__How many__ balls __are there__ ? – __Twenty-one__

Now stick the flower on your English Certificate!

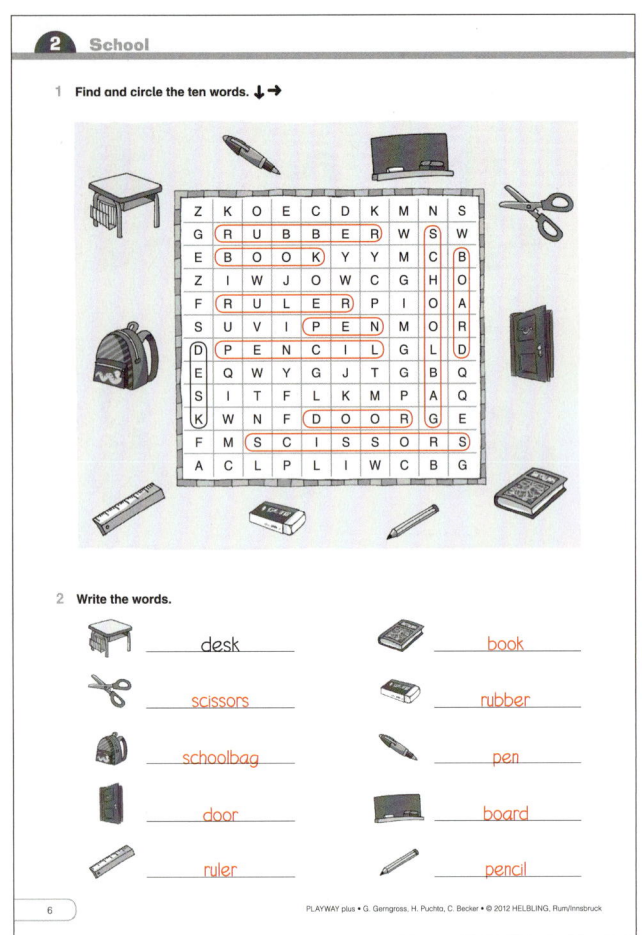

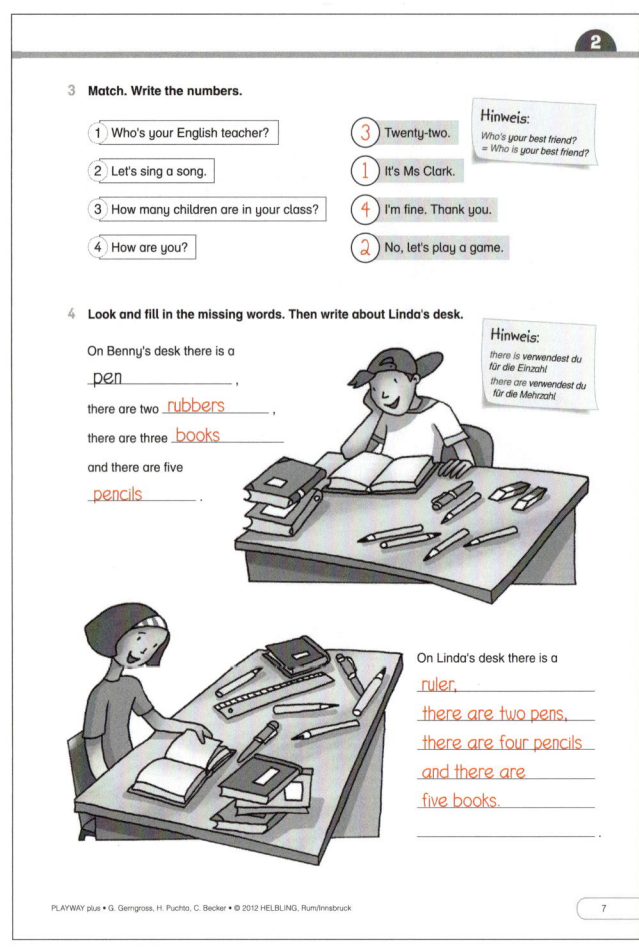

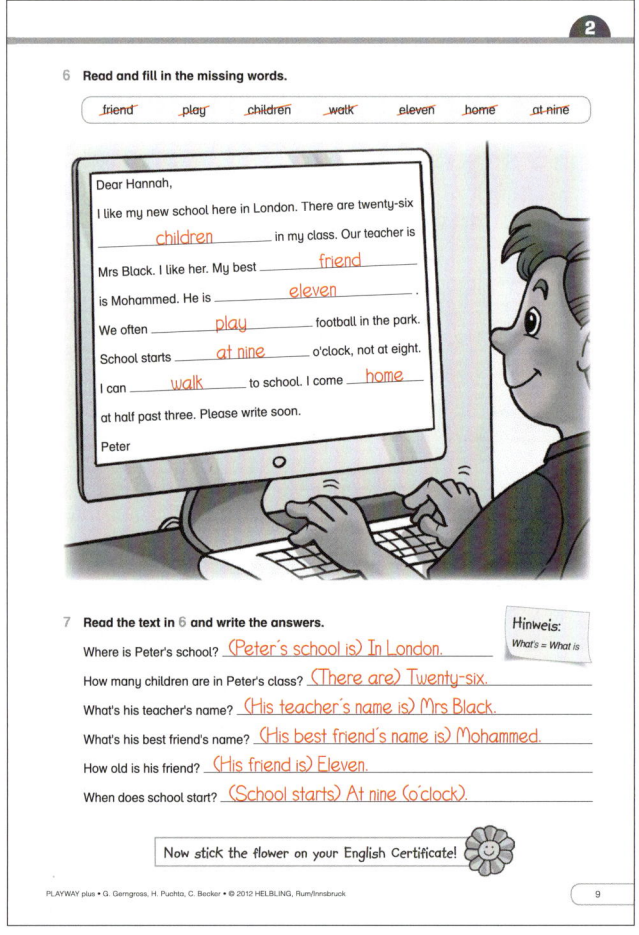

# 2  Lösungen

## 2  School

**1  Find and circle the ten words. ↓ →**

```
Z K O E C D K M N S
G R U B B E R W S W
E B O O K Y Y M C B
Z I W J O W C G H O
F R U L E R P I O A
S U V I P E N M O R
D P E N C I L G L D
E Q W Y G J T G B Q
S I T F L K M P A Q
K W N F D O O R G E
F M S C I S S O R S
A C L P L I W C B G
```

**2  Write the words.**

desk — book
scissors — rubber
schoolbag — pen
door — board
ruler — pencil

**3  Match. Write the numbers.**

1 Who's your English teacher? — 3 Twenty-two.
2 Let's sing a song. — 1 It's Ms Clark.
3 How many children are in your class? — 4 I'm fine. Thank you.
4 How are you? — 2 No, let's play a game.

*Hinweis: Who's your best friend? = Who is your best friend?*

**4  Look and fill in the missing words. Then write about Linda's desk.**

On Benny's desk there is a pen,
there are two rubbers,
there are three books
and there are five pencils.

*Hinweis: there is verwendest du für die Einzahl. there are verwendest du für die Mehrzahl*

On Linda's desk there is a ruler, there are two pens, there are four pencils and there are five books.

**5  Write the sentences.   She is ... / He is ...**

taking his bag · checking her watch · having a glass of milk
putting books in her bag · walking to school · reading a book

She is reading a book.
He is walking to school.
He is having a glass of milk.
She is putting books in her bag.
She is checking her watch.
He is taking his bag.

**6  Read and fill in the missing words.**

friend · play · children · walk · eleven · home · at nine

Dear Hannah,
I like my new school here in London. There are twenty-six children in my class. Our teacher is Mrs Black. I like her. My best friend is Mohammed. He is eleven. We often play football in the park. School starts at nine o'clock, not at eight. I can walk to school. I come home at half past three. Please write soon.
Peter

**7  Read the text in 6 and write the answers.**

*Hinweis: What's = What is*

Where is Peter's school? (Peter's school is) In London.
How many children are in Peter's class? (There are) Twenty-six.
What's his teacher's name? (His teacher's name is) Mrs Black.
What's his best friend's name? (His best friend's name is) Mohammed.
How old is his friend? (His friend is) Eleven.
When does school start? (School starts) At nine (o'clock).

Now stick the flower on your English Certificate!

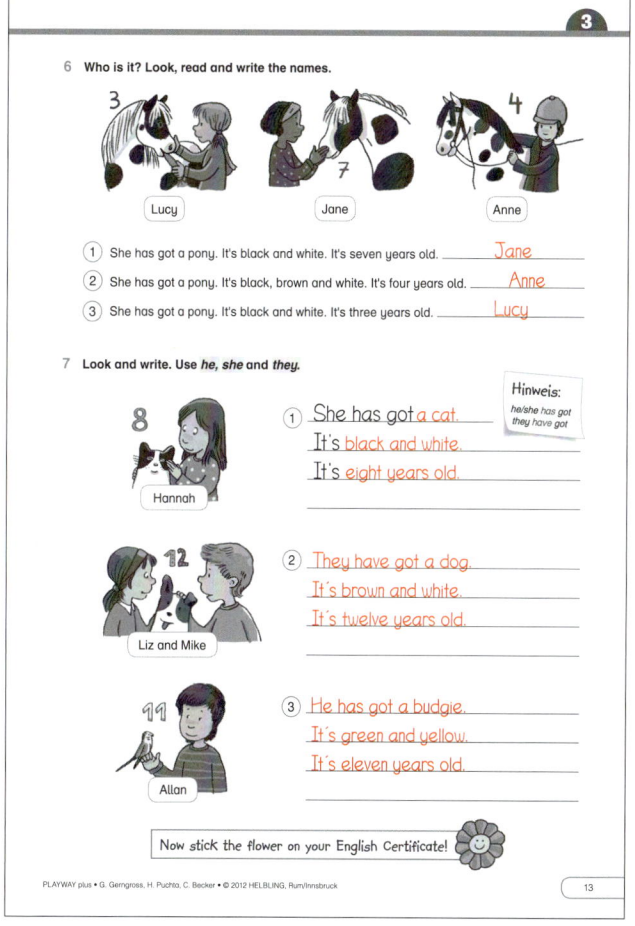

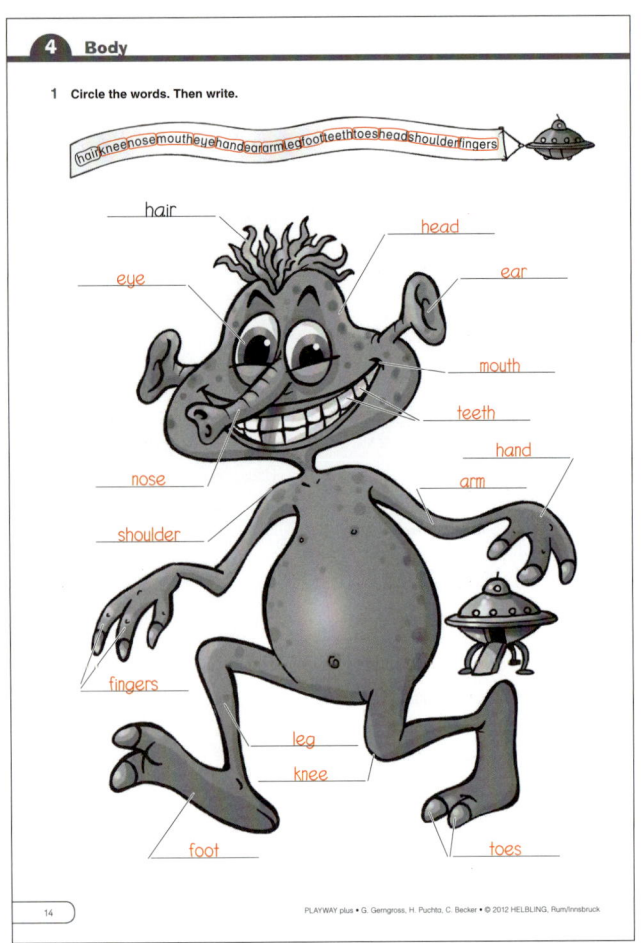

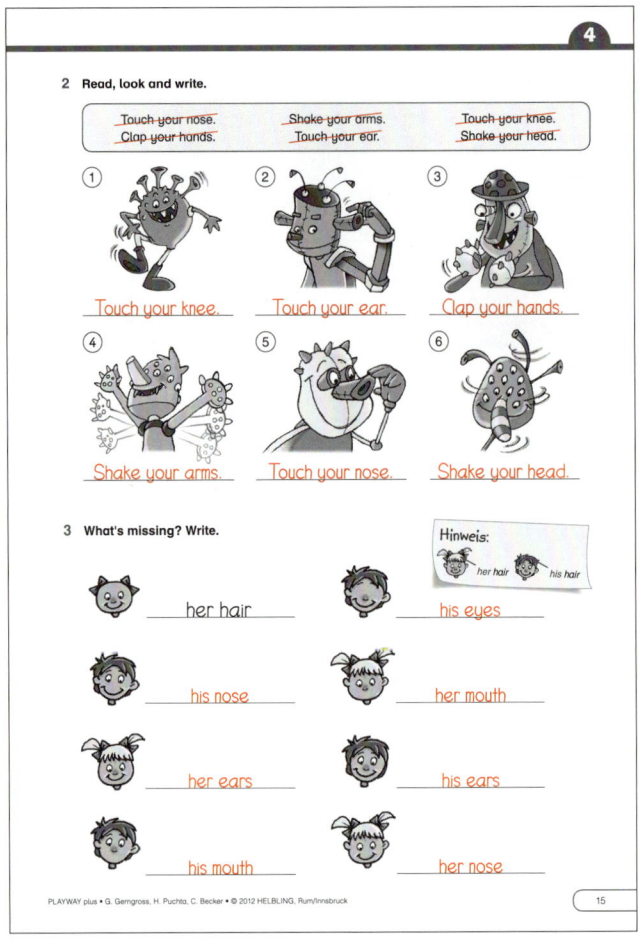

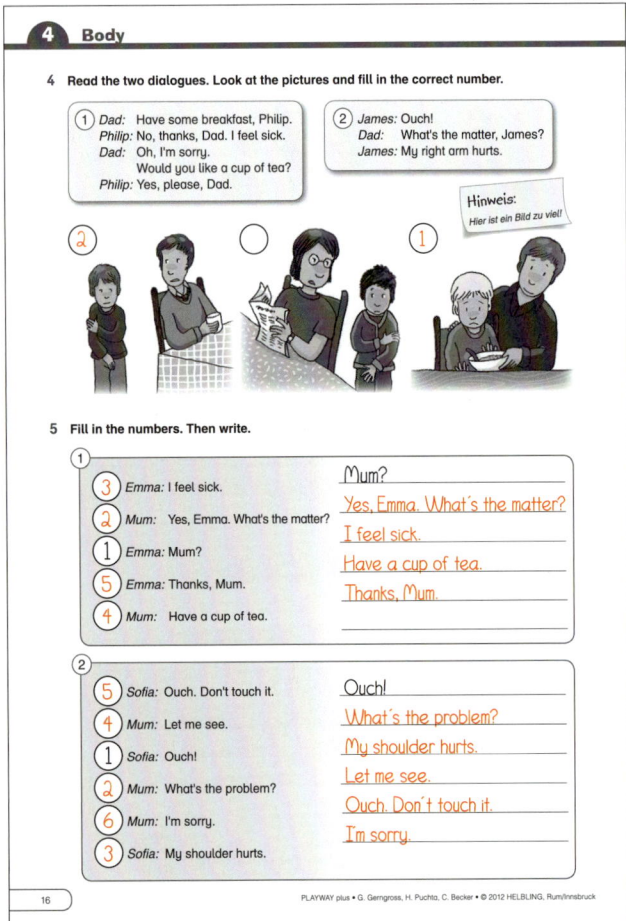

PLAYWAY plus – LÖSUNGSHEFT • G. Gerngross, H. Puchta, C. Becker • © 2012 HELBLING, Rum/Innsbruck

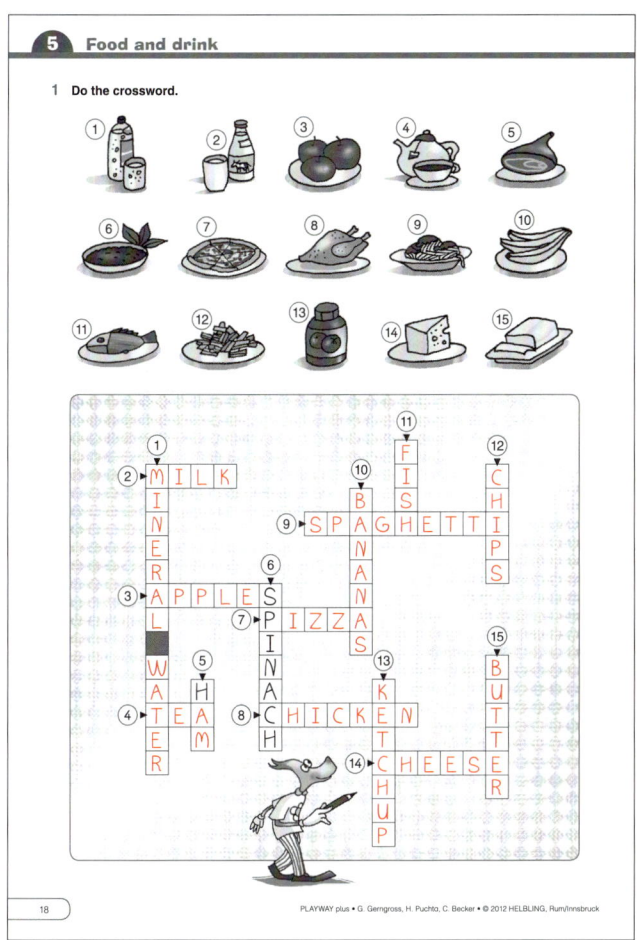

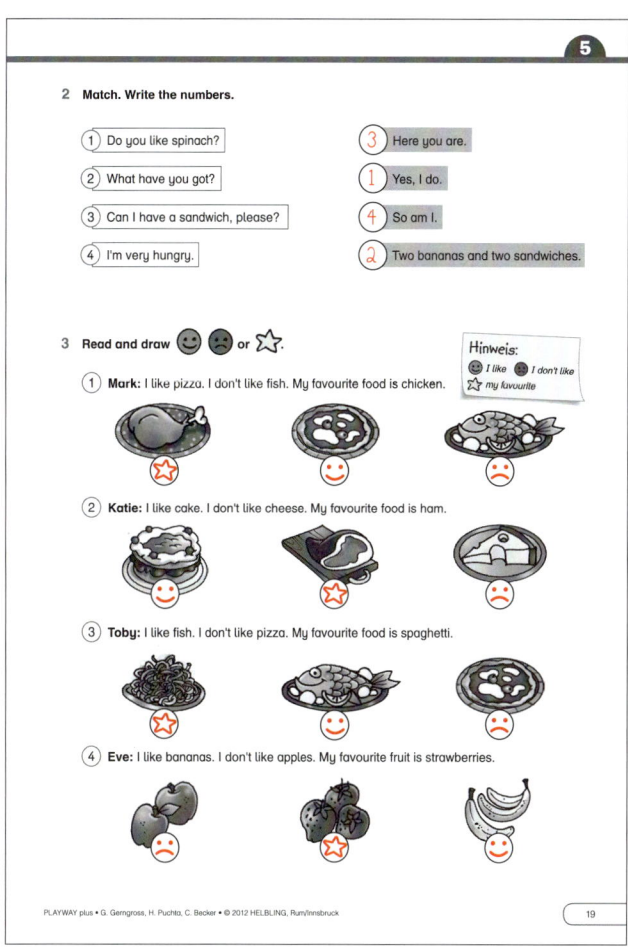

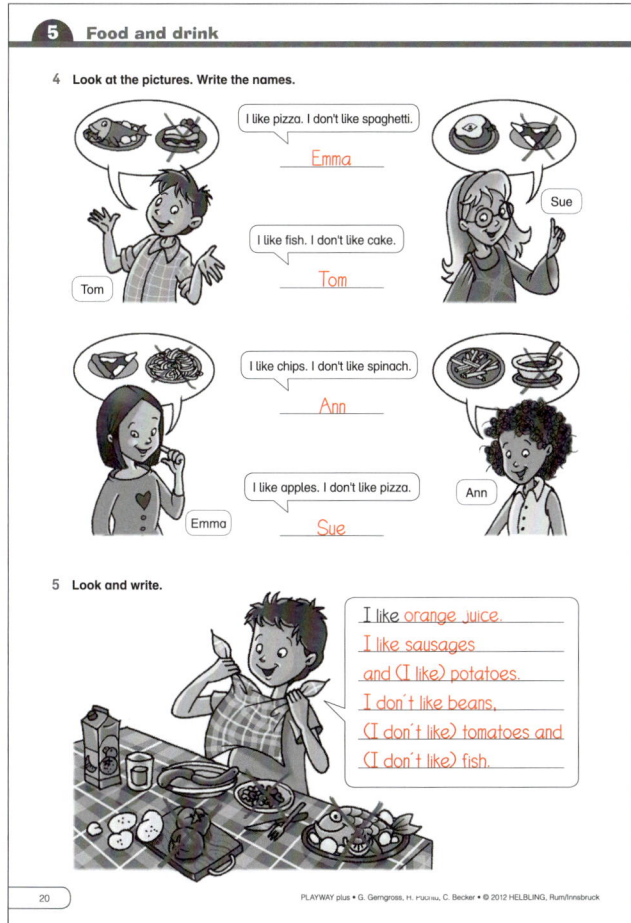

## 6 At the restaurant

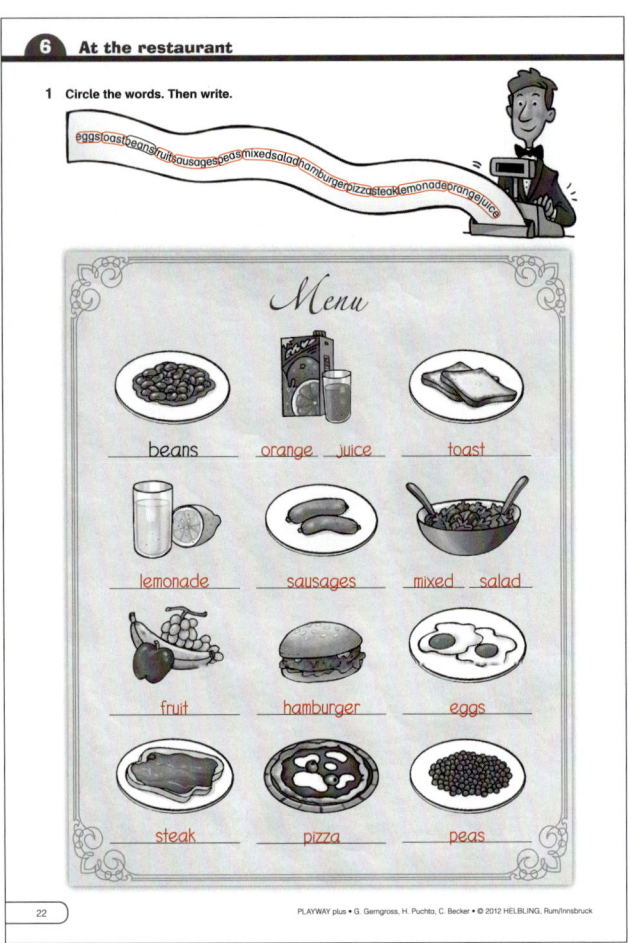

**1 Circle the words. Then write.**

eggs toast beans fruit sausages peas mixed salad hamburger pizza steak lemonade orange juice

*Menu*

beans | orange juice | toast
lemonade | sausages | mixed salad
fruit | hamburger | eggs
steak | pizza | peas

**2 Look and write** *Linda, Benny, Mum* or *Dad.*

I'm having a hamburger, a mixed salad and cola.

I'm having steak, peas and orange juice.

I'm having sausages, peas and lemonade.

I'm having a mixed salad, pizza and mineral water.

Dad    Benny    Mum    Linda

**3 Read. Then complete the sentences.**

| | hamburgers | fish and chips | pizza | sausages | mixed salad |
|---|---|---|---|---|---|
| Noah | ☺ | ☹ | ☺ | ☺ | ☹ |
| Kirsten | ☹ | ☺ | ☺ | ☹ | ☺ |

① Noah likes hamburgers. He doesn't like fish and chips.
He likes pizza.
He likes sausages.
He doesn't like mixed salad.

② Kirsten doesn't like hamburgers. She likes fish and chips.
She likes pizza.
She doesn't like sausages.
She likes mixed salad.

## 6 At the restaurant

**4 Read and complete the dialogues.**

orange juice   pizza   mineral water   thank you   chips
Here   Would   steak   drink   eat

What would you like to eat?

*Hinweis:*
*I'd like = I would like*
*we'd like = we would like*

I'd like steak and chips, please.

What would you like to drink?

I'd like a pizza, please.

We'd like mineral water and an orange juice, please.

Here you are.

Would you like a dessert?

Thank you.

No, thank you.

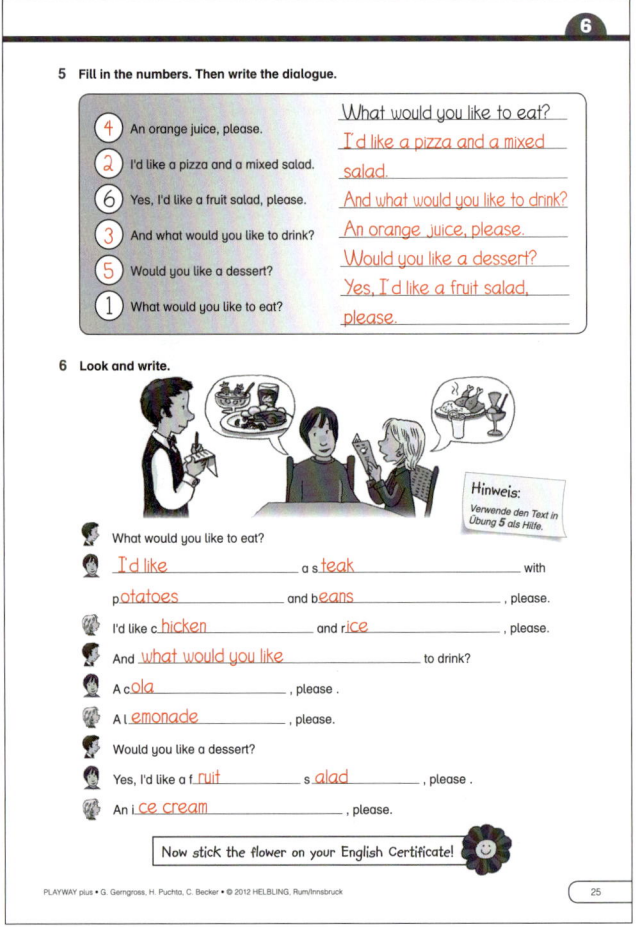

**5 Fill in the numbers. Then write the dialogue.**

4 An orange juice, please.
2 I'd like a pizza and a mixed salad.
6 Yes, I'd like a fruit salad, please.
3 And what would you like to drink?
5 Would you like a dessert?
1 What would you like to eat?

What would you like to eat?
I'd like a pizza and a mixed salad.
And what would you like to drink?
An orange juice, please.
Would you like a dessert?
Yes, I'd like a fruit salad, please.

**6 Look and write.**

*Hinweis:*
*Verwende den Text in Übung 5 als Hilfe.*

What would you like to eat?
I'd like a steak with potatoes and beans, please.
I'd like chicken and rice, please.
And what would you like to drink?
A cola, please.
A lemonade, please.
Would you like a dessert?
Yes, I'd like a fruit salad, please.
An ice cream, please.

Now stick the flower on your English Certificate! ☺

## 7  Family and feelings

**1  Write the words.**

> grandpa · sister · grandma · mum · brother
> brother · grandma · dad · grandpa · sister

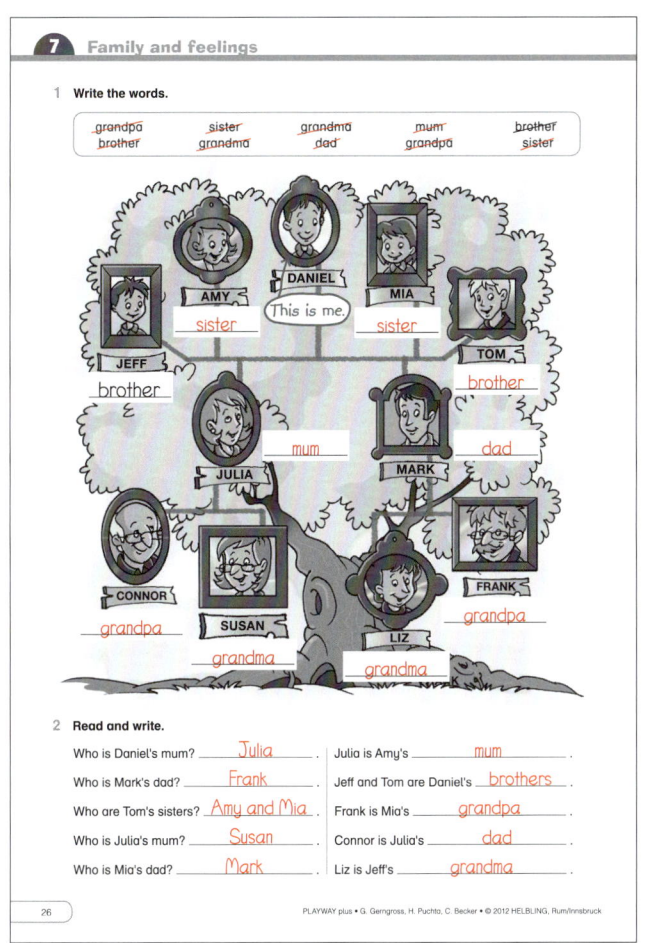

AMY — sister
DANIEL — This is me.
MIA — sister
JEFF — brother
TOM — brother
JULIA — mum
MARK — dad
CONNOR — grandpa
SUSAN — grandma
LIZ — grandma
FRANK — grandpa

**2  Read and write.**

| | |
|---|---|
| Who is Daniel's mum? __Julia__ . | Julia is Amy's __mum__ . |
| Who is Mark's dad? __Frank__ . | Jeff and Tom are Daniel's __brothers__ . |
| Who are Tom's sisters? __Amy and Mia__ . | Frank is Mia's __grandpa__ . |
| Who is Julia's mum? __Susan__ . | Connor is Julia's __dad__ . |
| Who is Mia's dad? __Mark__ . | Liz is Jeff's __grandma__ . |

---

**3  Read and fill in the numbers.**

Hinweis: there's = there is

1. Hi, my name is Leah. In my family there's my mum, my two brothers, my sister Patricia and me.
2. Hi, I'm Holly. In my family there's my brother Christopher, my grandpa, my mum and me.
3. Hi, I'm Jessica. In my family there's my dad, my mum, my grandpa, my grandma and me.
4. Hi, I'm Grace. In my family there's my grandma Rose, my grandma Eileen, my dad, my mum, my sister and me.

---

## 7  Family and feelings

**4  Write the words.**

> pyaph · das · ridet · yagnr · draces

angry · happy · scared · tired · sad

**5  Read the story. Look at the pictures and fill in the numbers.**

1.
Dad:  Are you sad, Simon?
Simon:  No, I'm scared.
Dad:  What's the problem?

2.
Simon:  There's a dog in our garden.
Dad:  A dog?
Simon:  Yes.

3.
Dad:  OK, I'll go and check.
Dad goes out …

4.
… and comes back very fast.
Simon:  Dad, are you scared too?
Dad:  Yes, I'm scared.

5.
Dad:  The dog is very big and angry.

---

**6  Fill in the numbers. Then write the dialogue.**

| 3 | What's the problem? |
| 5 | Would you like some bread with ham? |
| 1 | Are you angry? |
| 6 | Yes, please. |
| 2 | No, I'm not. |
| 4 | I'm hungry. |

Are you angry?
No, I'm not.
What's the problem?
I'm hungry.
Would you like some bread with ham?
Yes, please.

**7  Read and complete the sentences.**

> nine · he · she · her · his · is · got

My name __is__ Gabriel. I'm __nine__ .
I've __got__ a brother and a sister.
__His__ name is John and __her__ name is Jennifer.
__He__ is six and __she__ is three.

Hinweis: Wörter am Satzanfang werden mit großen Anfangsbuchstaben geschrieben.

**8  Look and write.**

My name is Kate. I'm ten.
I've got a sister and a brother.
Her name is Sarah
and his name is Rick.
She is seven and he is five.

Kate 10
Sarah 7
Rick 5

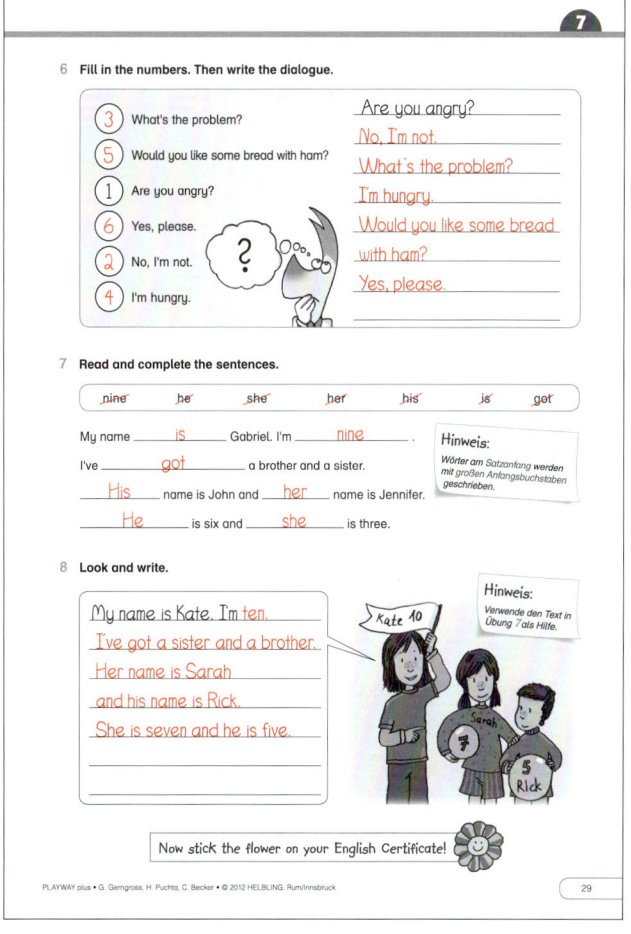

Hinweis: Verwende den Text in Übung 7 als Hilfe.

Now stick the flower on your English Certificate!

---

**1  Write.**

window   table   chair   wardrobe   lamp   stairs   bed   sofa

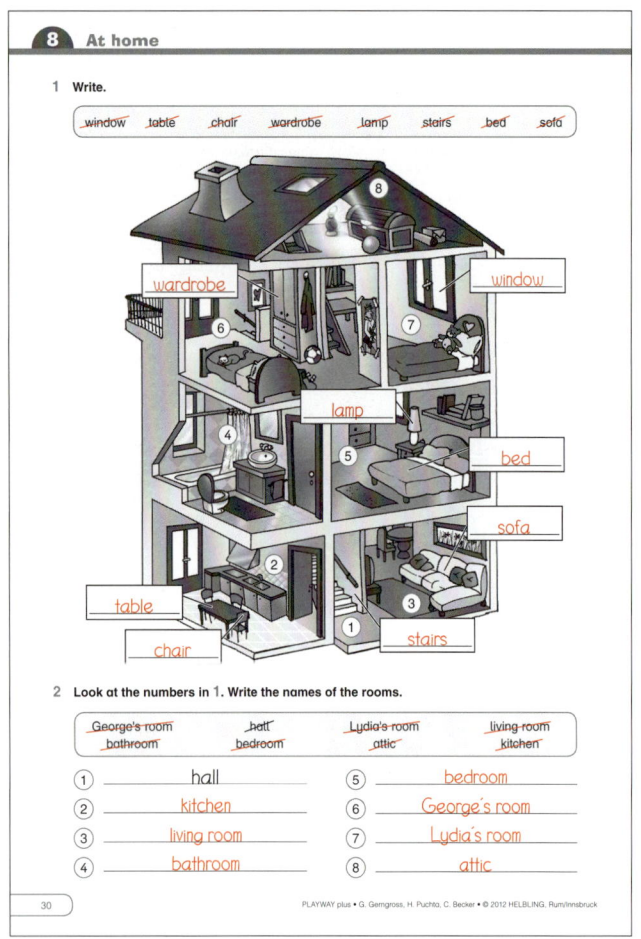

wardrobe   window   lamp   bed   sofa   table   chair   stairs

**2  Look at the numbers in 1. Write the names of the rooms.**

George's room   hall   Lydia's room   living room
bathroom   bedroom   attic   kitchen

1  hall
2  kitchen
3  living room
4  bathroom
5  bedroom
6  George's room
7  Lydia's room
8  attic

**3  Look and match.**

in   on   under   in front of   next to   behind

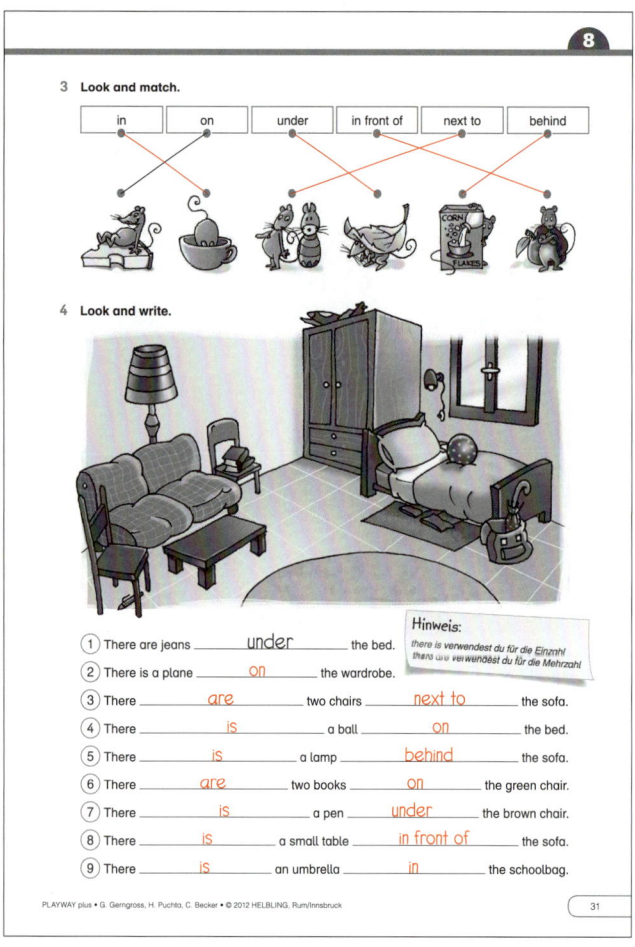

**4  Look and write.**

1  There are jeans __under__ the bed.
2  There is a plane __on__ the wardrobe.
3  There __are__ two chairs __next to__ the sofa.
4  There __is__ a ball __on__ the bed.
5  There __is__ a lamp __behind__ the sofa.
6  There __are__ two books __on__ the green chair.
7  There __is__ a pen __under__ the brown chair.
8  There __is__ a small table __in front of__ the sofa.
9  There __is__ an umbrella __in__ the schoolbag.

**Hinweis:**
*there is verwendest du für die Einzahl*
*there are verwendest du für die Mehrzahl*

**5  Read and fill in the missing words.**

is   interesting   favourite   big   things

Hi Anna,
London is great. There are lots of __things__ to do.
My __favourite__ place is the London Eye.
From up there you can see how __big__ London is.
There is also a great museum, the Natural History Museum.
There __is__ a big fossil of the
Brontosaurus and many other __interesting__ things.
Love,
Ella

LONDON EYE

**6  Write the sentences.**

Take off your shoes, please.   Where's the bathroom, please?
What are you doing in the kitchen?   Let's go to the attic.

Take off your shoes, please.

Let's go to the attic.

Where's the bathroom, please?

What are you doing in the kitchen?

**7  Read the text and draw.**

In Linda's room the desk is in front of the window with the yellow curtains. There is a green chair in front of the desk. On the desk there is a lamp. The bed is opposite the desk. The wardrobe is behind the door. There is a small table between the door and the window with the blue curtains. On the bed there is a teddy bear. The schoolbag is under the bed.

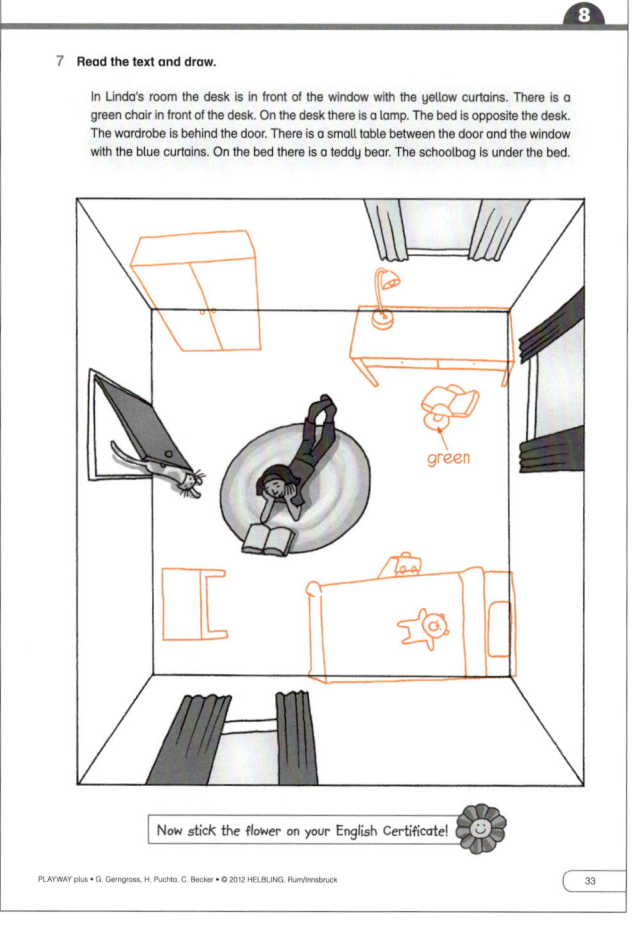

green

Now stick the flower on your English Certificate!

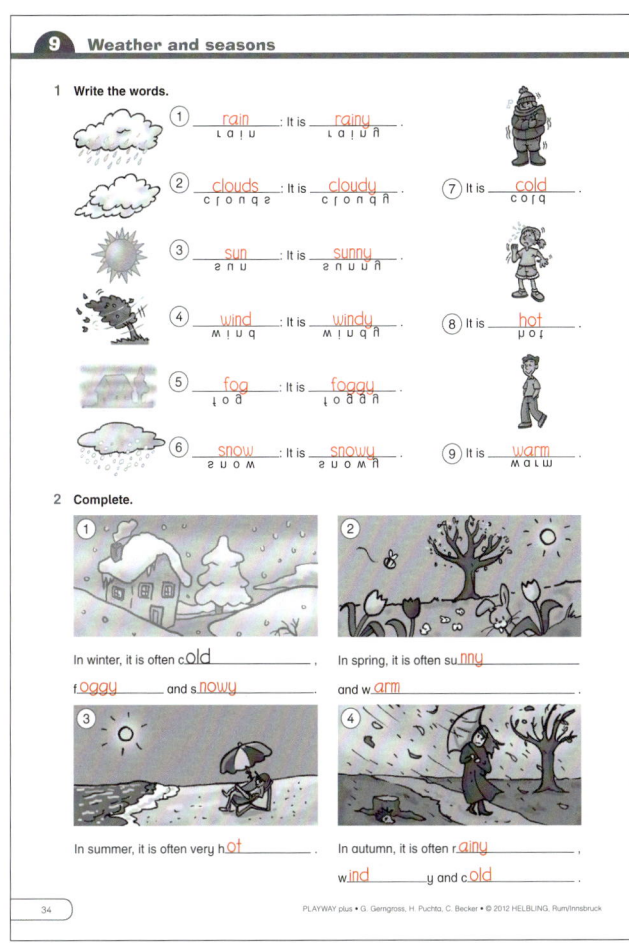

**9  Weather and seasons**

**1  Write the words.**

1. rain : It is rainy .
   ɹɐıu / ɹɐıuʎ
2. clouds : It is cloudy
   cloudʂ / cloudʎ
3. sun : It is sunny
   ʂun / ʂunnʎ
4. wind : It is windy
   wınd / wındʎ
5. fog : It is foggy
   foɓ / foɓɓʎ
6. snow : It is snowy
   ʂnow / ʂnowʎ

7. It is cold
   cold
8. It is hot
   hoʇ
9. It is warm
   waɹɯ

**2  Complete.**

1. In winter, it is often cold
   foggy and snowy .
2. In spring, it is often sunny
   and warm .
3. In summer, it is often very hot .
4. In autumn, it is often rainy ,
   windy and cold .

PLAYWAY plus • G. Gerngross, H. Puchta, C. Becker • © 2012 HELBLING, Rum/Innsbruck

**3  What's the weather like today? Look and complete.**

1. JANUARY 12 — MOSCOW -15°C
2. JUNE 26 — LONDON 23°C
3. JULY 30 — PARIS 22°C
4. AUGUST 21 — VIENNA 31°C
5. OCTOBER 18 — NEW YORK 10°C
6. DECEMBER 9 — SAN FRANCISCO 12°C

1. **JANUARY 12** What's the weather like today in Moscow?
   It's snowy and cold.
2. **JUNE 26** What's the weather like today in London?
   It's sunny and warm .
3. **JULY 30** What's the weather like today in Paris?
   It's cloudy and warm.
4. **AUGUST 21** What's the weather like today in Vienna?
   It's sunny and hot.
5. **OCTOBER 18** What's the weather like today in New York?
   It's rainy and cold.
6. **DECEMBER 9** What's the weather like today in San Francisco?
   It's foggy and cold.

PLAYWAY plus • G. Gerngross, H. Puchta, C. Becker • © 2012 HELBLING, Rum/Innsbruck

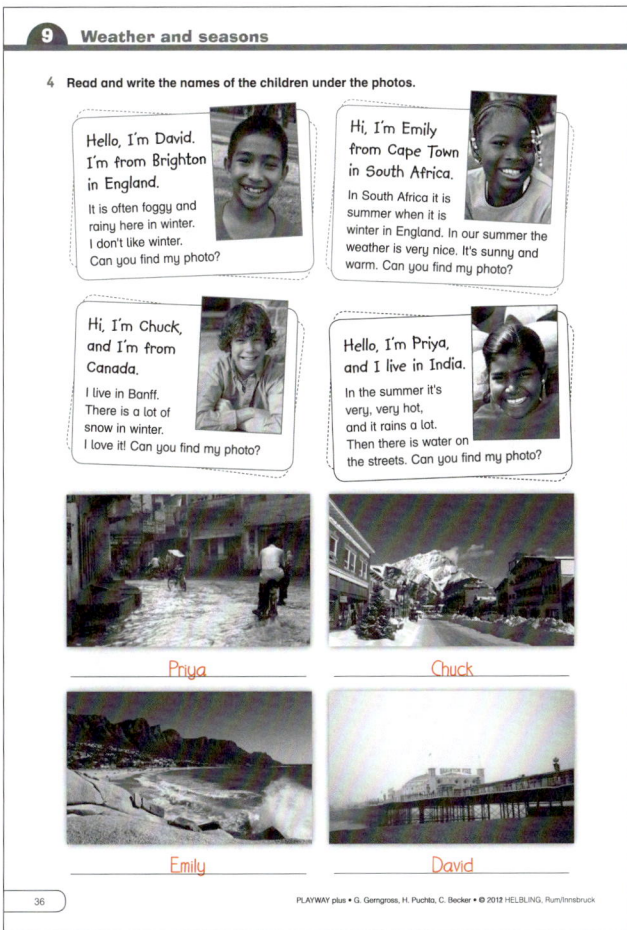

**9  Weather and seasons**

**4  Read and write the names of the children under the photos.**

Hello, I'm David. I'm from Brighton in England.
It is often foggy and rainy here in winter. I don't like winter. Can you find my photo?

Hi, I'm Emily from Cape Town in South Africa.
In South Africa it is summer when it is winter in England. In our summer the weather is very nice. It's sunny and warm. Can you find my photo?

Hi, I'm Chuck, and I'm from Canada.
I live in Banff. There is a lot of snow in winter. I love it! Can you find my photo?

Hello, I'm Priya, and I live in India.
In the summer it's very, very hot, and it rains a lot. Then there is water on the streets. Can you find my photo?

Priya   Chuck

Emily   David

PLAYWAY plus • G. Gerngross, H. Puchta, C. Becker • © 2012 HELBLING, Rum/Innsbruck

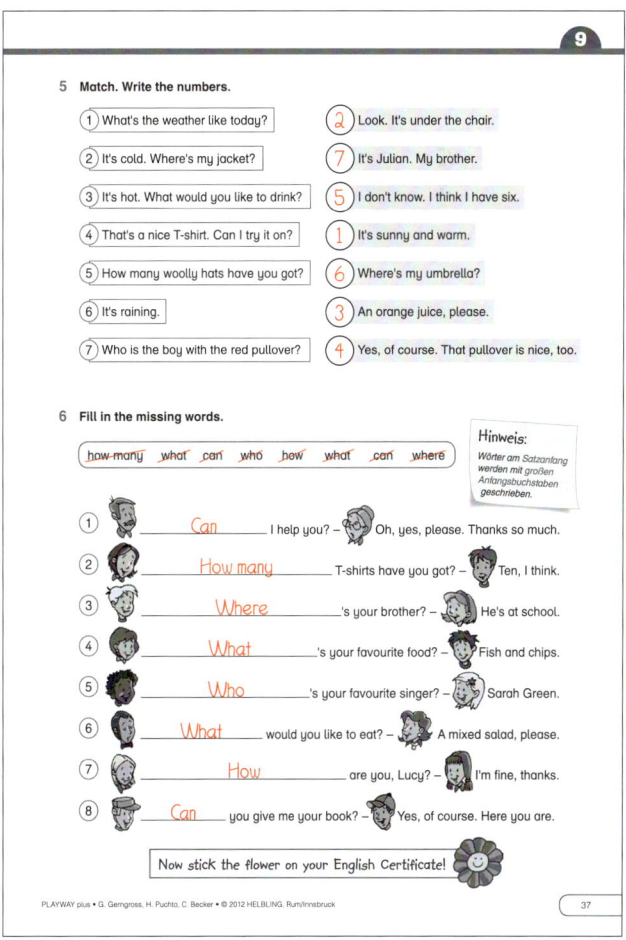

**5  Match. Write the numbers.**

1. What's the weather like today? — 1  It's sunny and warm.
2. It's cold. Where's my jacket? — 6  Where's my umbrella?
3. It's hot. What would you like to drink? — 3  An orange juice, please.
4. That's a nice T-shirt. Can I try it on? — 4  Yes, of course. That pullover is nice, too.
5. How many woolly hats have you got? — 5  I don't know. I think I have six.
6. It's raining. — 2  Look. It's under the chair.
7. Who is the boy with the red pullover? — 7  It's Julian. My brother.

**6  Fill in the missing words.**

how-many  what  can  who  how  what  can  where

*Hinweis:*
*Wörter am Satzanfang werden mit großen Anfangsbuchstaben geschrieben.*

1. Can I help you? – Oh, yes, please. Thanks so much.
2. How many T-shirts have you got? – Ten, I think.
3. Where 's your brother? – He's at school.
4. What 's your favourite food? – Fish and chips.
5. Who 's your favourite singer? – Sarah Green.
6. What would you like to eat? – A mixed salad, please.
7. How are you, Lucy? – I'm fine, thanks.
8. Can you give me your book? – Yes, of course. Here you are.

Now stick the flower on your English Certificate!

PLAYWAY plus • G. Gerngross, H. Puchta, C. Becker • © 2012 HELBLING, Rum/Innsbruck

PLAYWAY plus – LÖSUNGSHEFT • G. Gerngross, H. Puchta, C. Becker • © 2012 HELBLING, Rum/Innsbruck

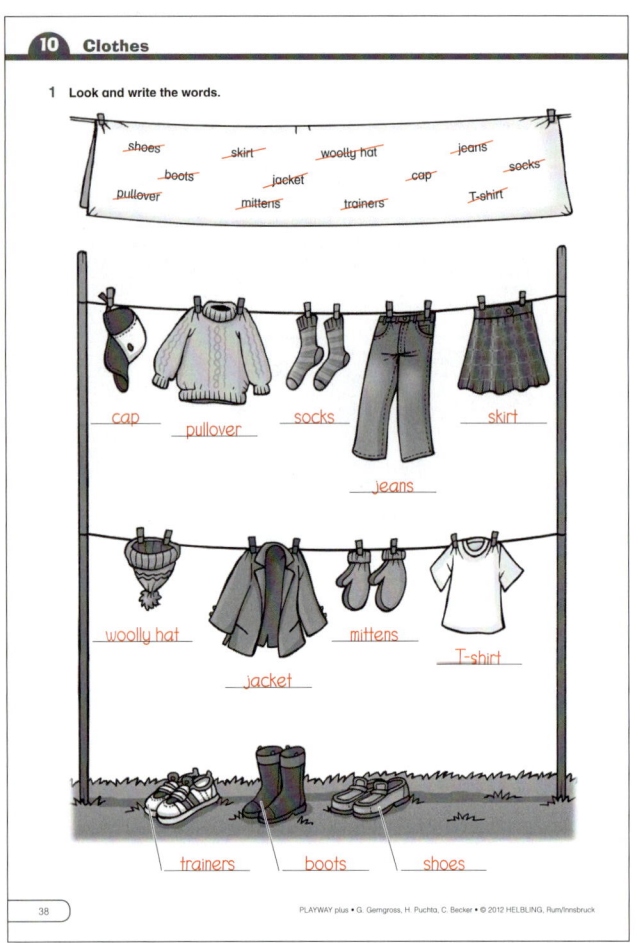

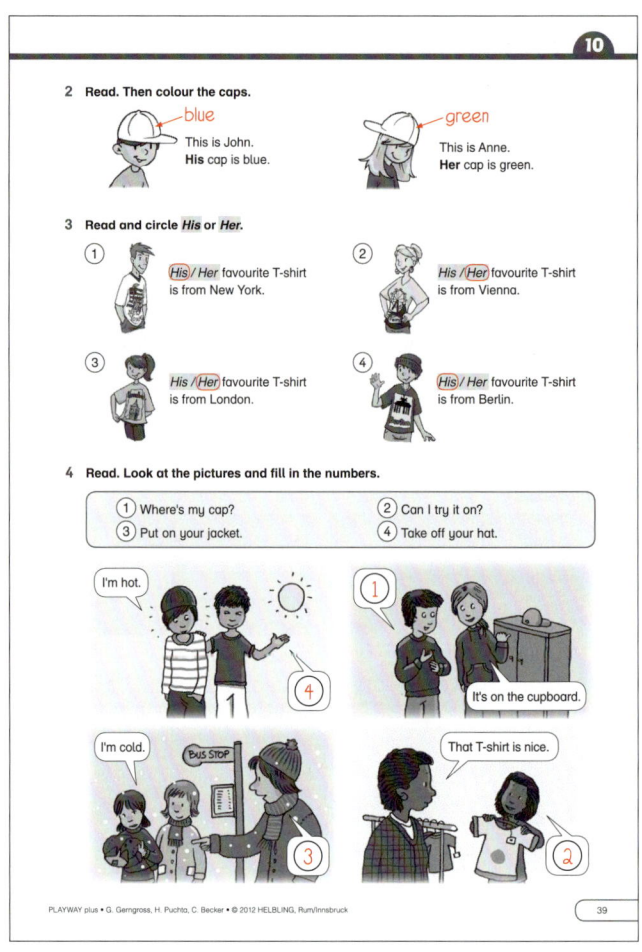

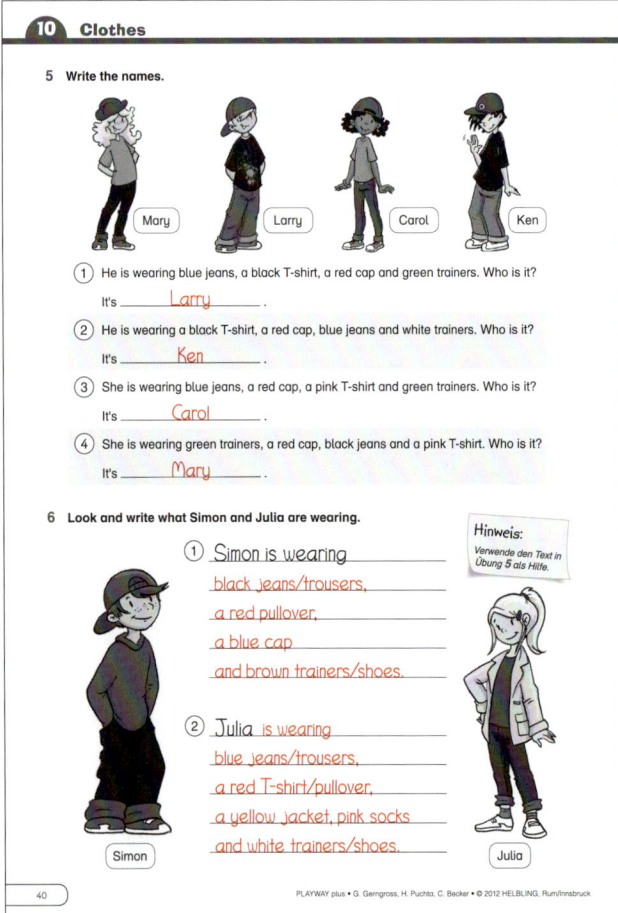

## Page 38 — Clothes

**10** Clothes

**1 Look and write the words.**

shoes · skirt · woolly hat · jeans
boots · jacket · cap · socks
pullover · mittens · trainers · T-shirt

cap · pullover · socks · skirt

jeans

woolly hat · mittens · T-shirt

jacket

trainers · boots · shoes

38

PLAYWAY plus • G. Gerngross, H. Puchta, C. Becker • © 2012 HELBLING, Rum/Innsbruck

## Page 39

**10**

**2 Read. Then colour the caps.**

blue — This is John. **His** cap is blue.

green — This is Anne. **Her** cap is green.

**3 Read and circle *His* or *Her*.**

① *His* / Her favourite T-shirt is from New York.

② His / *Her* favourite T-shirt is from Vienna.

③ His / *Her* favourite T-shirt is from London.

④ *His* / Her favourite T-shirt is from Berlin.

**4 Read. Look at the pictures and fill in the numbers.**

① Where's my cap?
② Can I try it on?
③ Put on your jacket.
④ Take off your hat.

I'm hot. — 4

1 — It's on the cupboard.

I'm cold. — BUS STOP — 3

That T-shirt is nice. — 2

39

PLAYWAY plus • G. Gerngross, H. Puchta, C. Becker • © 2012 HELBLING, Rum/Innsbruck

## Page 40 — Clothes

**10** Clothes

**5 Write the names.**

Mary · Larry · Carol · Ken

① He is wearing blue jeans, a black T-shirt, a red cap and green trainers. Who is it?
It's ____Larry____ .

② He is wearing a black T-shirt, a red cap, blue jeans and white trainers. Who is it?
It's ____Ken____ .

③ She is wearing blue jeans, a red cap, a pink T-shirt and green trainers. Who is it?
It's ____Carol____ .

④ She is wearing green trainers, a red cap, black jeans and a pink T-shirt. Who is it?
It's ____Mary____ .

**6 Look and write what Simon and Julia are wearing.**

① Simon is wearing
black jeans/trousers,
a red pullover,
a blue cap
and brown trainers/shoes.

② Julia is wearing
blue jeans/trousers,
a red T-shirt/pullover,
a yellow jacket, pink socks
and white trainers/shoes.

Hinweis:
Verwende den Text in Übung 5 als Hilfe.

Simon · Julia

40

PLAYWAY plus • G. Gerngross, H. Puchta, C. Becker • © 2012 HELBLING, Rum/Innsbruck

## Page 41

**10**

**7 Read and colour.**

yellow · blue · red · green

Hinweis:
his cap · her cap

Benny's favourite T-shirt is red.
There's a big crocodile on it.
It's green.

His favourite cap is blue.
There's a yellow star on it.

**8 Look and write.**

Linda's favourite T-shirt is pink.
There's a big flower on it.
It's yellow.
Her favourite cap is green.
There's a red butterfly on it.

Hinweis:
Verwende den Text in Übung 7 als Hilfe.

Now stick the flower on your English Certificate!

41

PLAYWAY plus • G. Gerngross, H. Puchta, C. Becker • © 2012 HELBLING, Rum/Innsbruck

**11** Shopping

**1** Look, count and write. Then write the names.

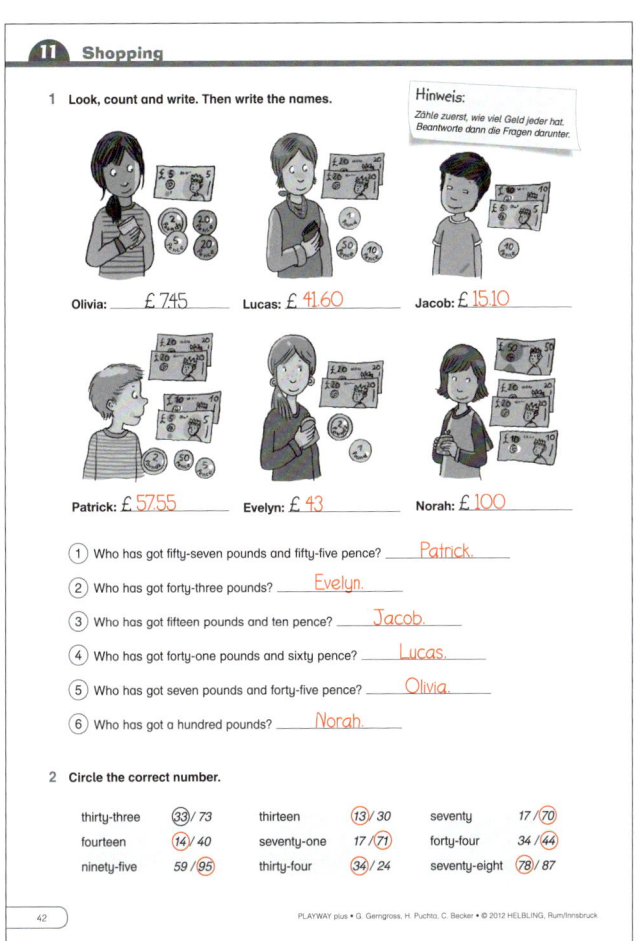

Hinweis:
Zähle zuerst, wie viel Geld jeder hat. Beantworte dann die Fragen darunter.

Olivia: £ 7.45    Lucas: £ 41.60    Jacob: £ 15.10

Patrick: £ 57.55    Evelyn: £ 43    Norah: £ 100

① Who has got fifty-seven pounds and fifty-five pence? __Patrick.__

② Who has got forty-three pounds? __Evelyn.__

③ Who has got fifteen pounds and ten pence? __Jacob.__

④ Who has got forty-one pounds and sixty pence? __Lucas.__

⑤ Who has got seven pounds and forty-five pence? __Olivia.__

⑥ Who has got a hundred pounds? __Norah.__

**2** Circle the correct number.

| | | | | | | |
|---|---|---|---|---|---|---|
| thirty-three | **33**/ 73 | thirteen | **13**/ 30 | seventy | 17 /**70** |
| fourteen | **14**/ 40 | seventy-one | 17 /**71** | forty-four | 34 /**44** |
| ninety-five | 59 /**95** | thirty-four | **34**/ 24 | seventy-eight | **78**/ 87 |

**3** Write the prices (p or £) for a kilo.

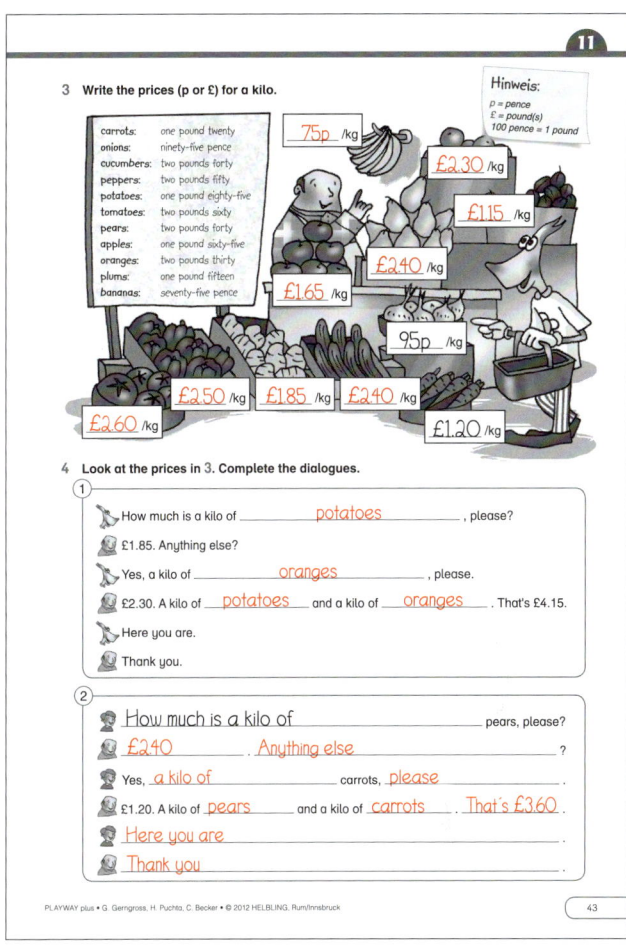

| | |
|---|---|
| carrots: | one pound twenty |
| onions: | ninety-five pence |
| cucumbers: | two pounds forty |
| peppers: | two pounds fifty |
| potatoes: | one pound eighty-five |
| tomatoes: | two pounds sixty |
| pears: | two pounds forty |
| apples: | one pound sixty-five |
| oranges: | two pounds thirty |
| plums: | one pound fifteen |
| bananas: | seventy-five pence |

Hinweis:
p = pence
£ = pound(s)
100 pence = 1 pound

75p /kg
£2.30 /kg
£1.15 /kg
£2.40 /kg
£1.65 /kg
95p /kg
£2.50 /kg  £1.85 /kg  £2.40 /kg
£2.60 /kg
£1.20 /kg

**4** Look at the prices in 3. Complete the dialogues.

①
How much is a kilo of __potatoes__, please?
£1.85. Anything else?
Yes, a kilo of __oranges__, please.
£2.30. A kilo of __potatoes__ and a kilo of __oranges__. That's £4.15.
Here you are.
Thank you.

②
__How much is a kilo of__ pears, please?
__£2.40. Anything else__ ?
Yes, __a kilo of__ carrots, __please__.
£1.20. A kilo of __pears__ and a kilo of __carrots__. __That's £3.60__.
__Here you are__.
__Thank you__.

**11** Shopping

**5** Read and write.

~~Yes, it's very good.~~    ~~Chicken and vegetables.~~
~~Sorry, Mum, I'm busy.~~    ~~I forgot the milk.~~

Can you go shopping for me, please?
It's nice, isn't it?

__Sorry, Mum, I'm busy.__    __Yes, it's very good.__

Where's the milk?
I'm so hungry. What's for dinner?

__I forgot the milk.__    __Chicken and vegetables.__

**6** Circle **is** or **are**.

① How much **is** /are the DVDs?    £10.85
② How much **is**/ are the green bike?    £85
③ How much **is**/ are the blue cap?    £6.99
④ How much is /**are** the jeans?    £45.40
⑤ How much is /**are** the books?    £12.50
⑥ How much is /**are** the shoes?    £19.50

Hinweis:
How much is ...? verwendest du für die Einzahl,
z.B.: How much is the pencil?
How much are ...? verwendest du für die Mehrzahl,
z.B.: How much are the pencils?
Achtung: "jeans" ist ein Mehrzahlwort

**7** Read and tick the correct picture. (✔)

Samuel often goes shopping for his mum. He buys fruit, eggs and milk.
He also buys bread, butter and cheese.

☐    ✔

**8** Look and write what Lilly buys for her mum.

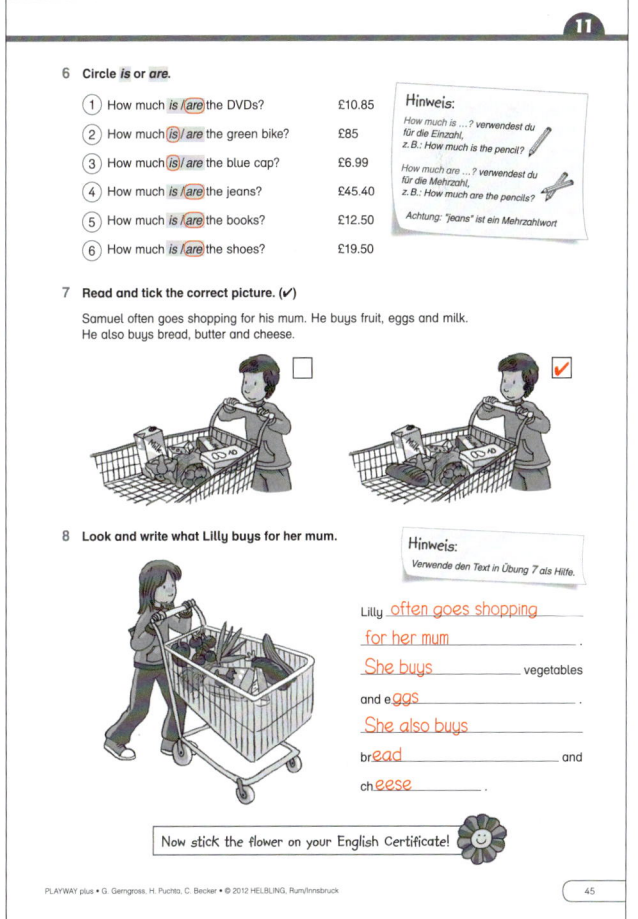

Hinweis:
Verwende den Text in Übung 7 als Hilfe.

Lilly __often goes shopping__
__for her mum__
__She buys__ vegetables
and e__ggs__
__She also buys__
br__ead__ and
ch__eese__

Now stick the flower on your English Certificate! ❀

**12** Free time

**1** Do the crossword.

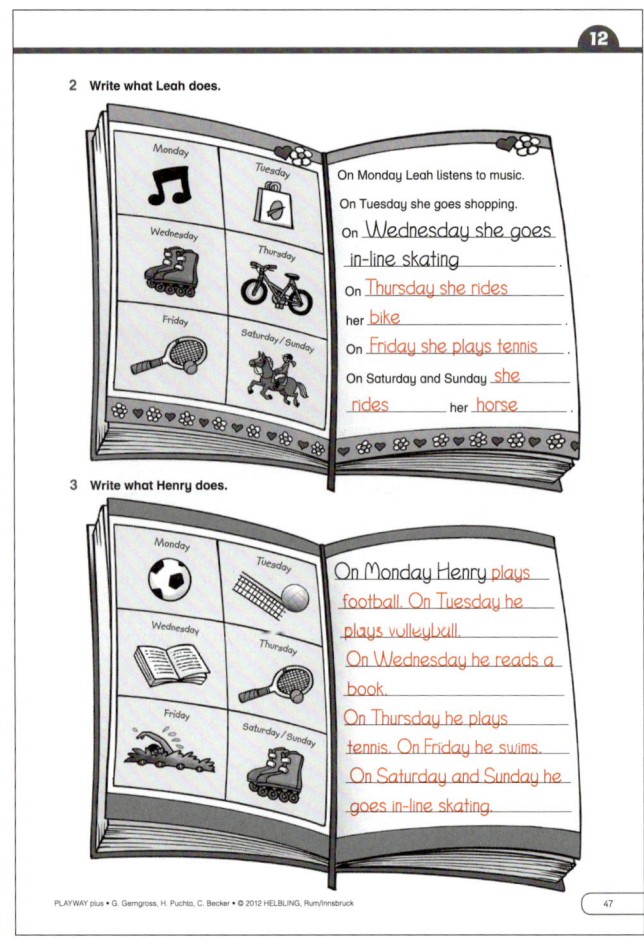

**2** Write what Leah does.

On Monday Leah listens to music.
On Tuesday she goes shopping.
On _Wednesday she goes_
_in-line skating_
On _Thursday she rides_
her _bike_
On _Friday she plays tennis_
On Saturday and Sunday _she_
_rides_ her _horse_

**3** Write what Henry does.

On Monday Henry _plays_
_football. On Tuesday he_
_plays volleyball._
_On Wednesday he reads a_
_book._
_On Thursday he plays_
_tennis. On Friday he swims._
_On Saturday and Sunday he_
_goes in-line skating._

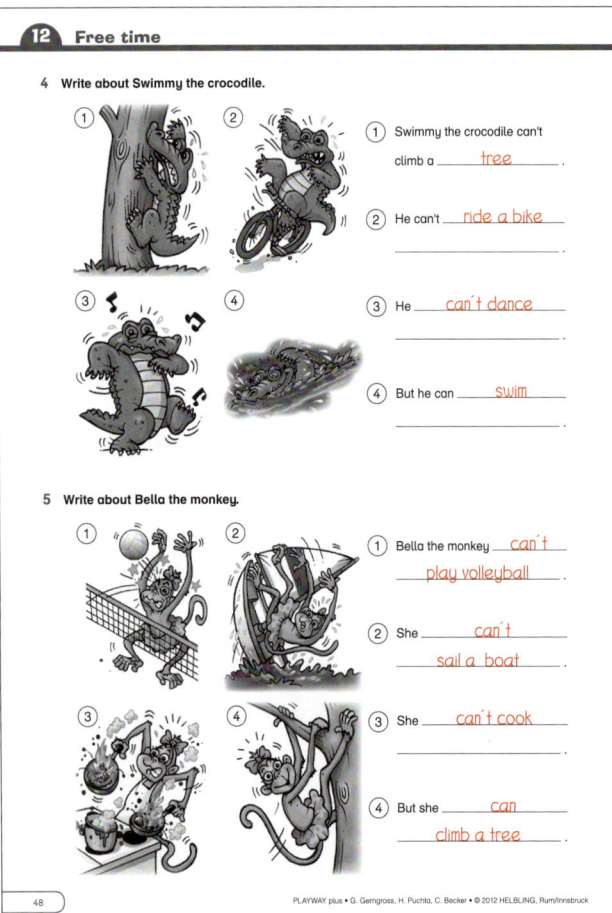

**12** Free time

**4** Write about Swimmy the crocodile.

① Swimmy the crocodile can't
climb a _tree_ .
② He can't _ride a bike_
③ He _can't dance_
④ But he can _swim_

**5** Write about Bella the monkey.

① Bella the monkey _can't_
_play volleyball_ .
② She _can't_
_sail a boat_
③ She _can't cook_
④ But she _can_
_climb a tree_

**6** Look at the pictures and complete the dialogues.

Yes, I can.    Can you    No, I can't.    Can you

Vicky: _Can you_ ride a horse?
Julia: _No, I can't._

Vicky: _Can you_ ride a unicycle?
Julia: _Yes, I can._

**7** Look and write the dialogues.

Ryan: _Can you sail a boat_ ?
Luke: _Yes, I can._

Ryan: _Can you play tennis_ ?
Luke: _No, I can't._

Now stick the flower on your English Certificate!

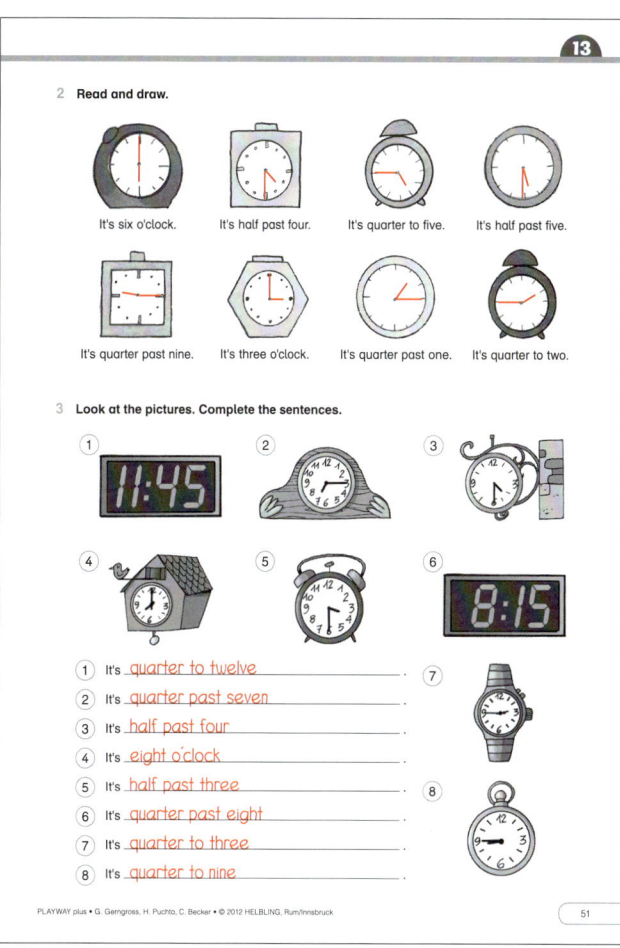

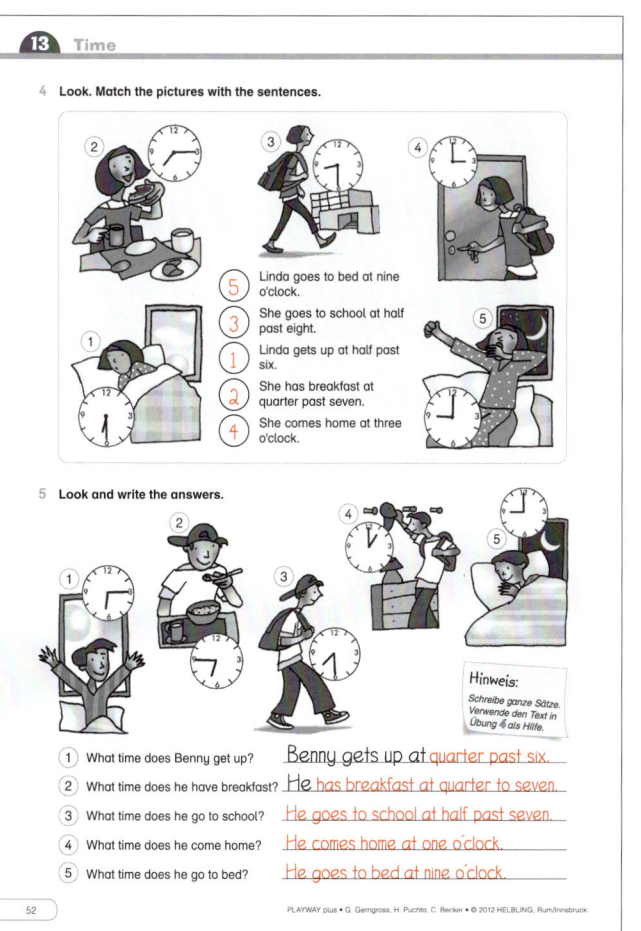

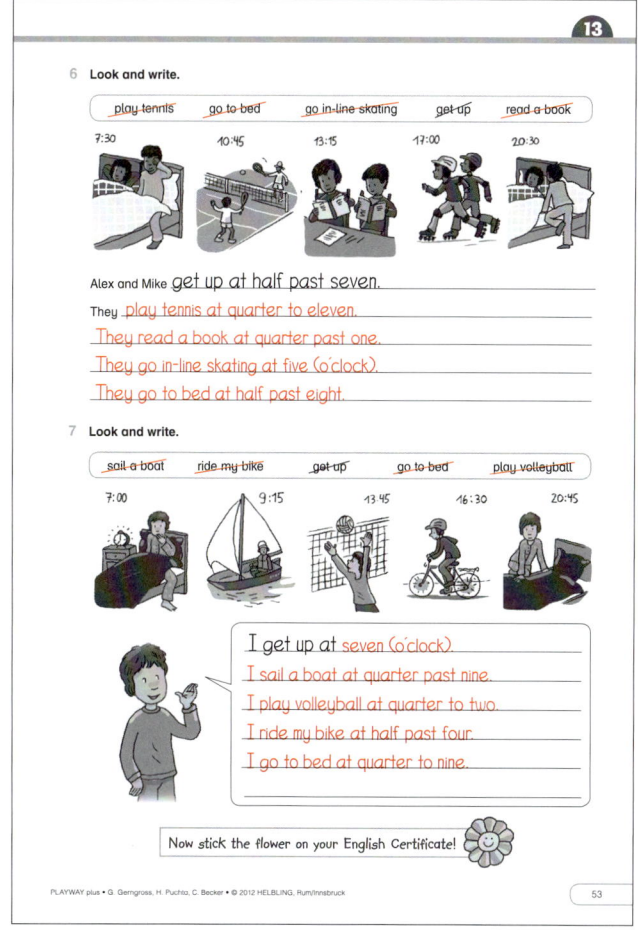

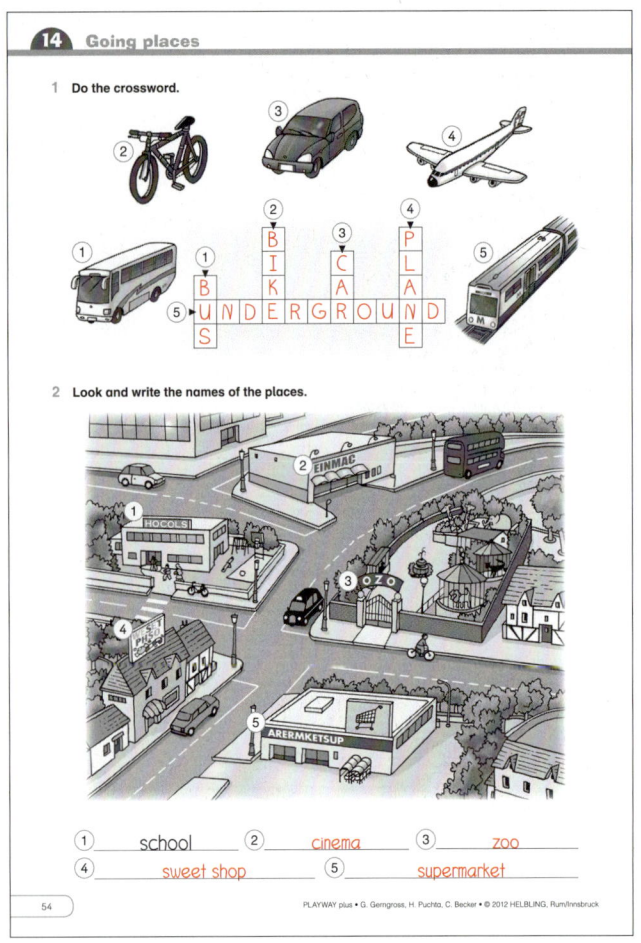

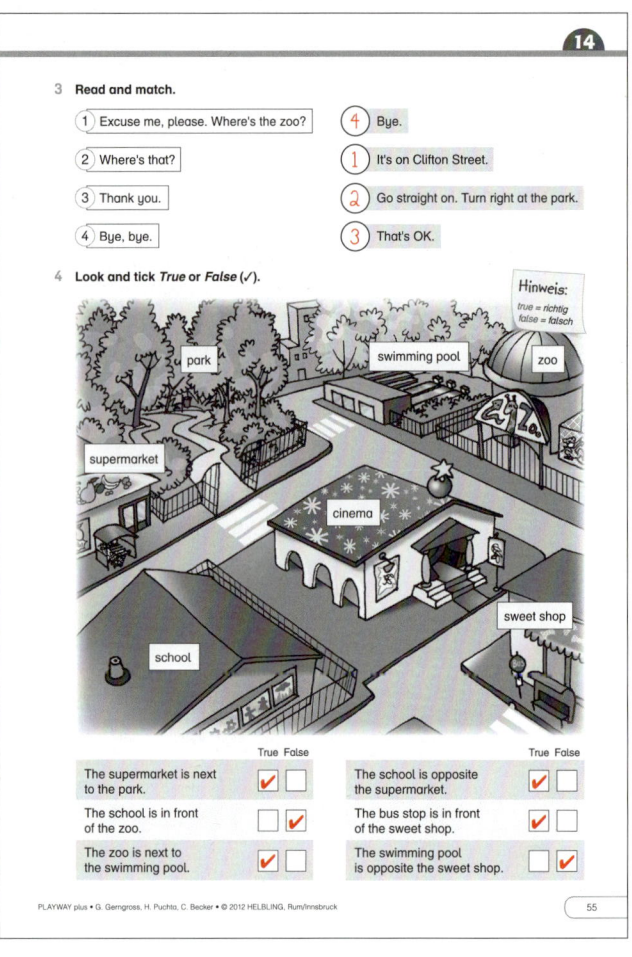

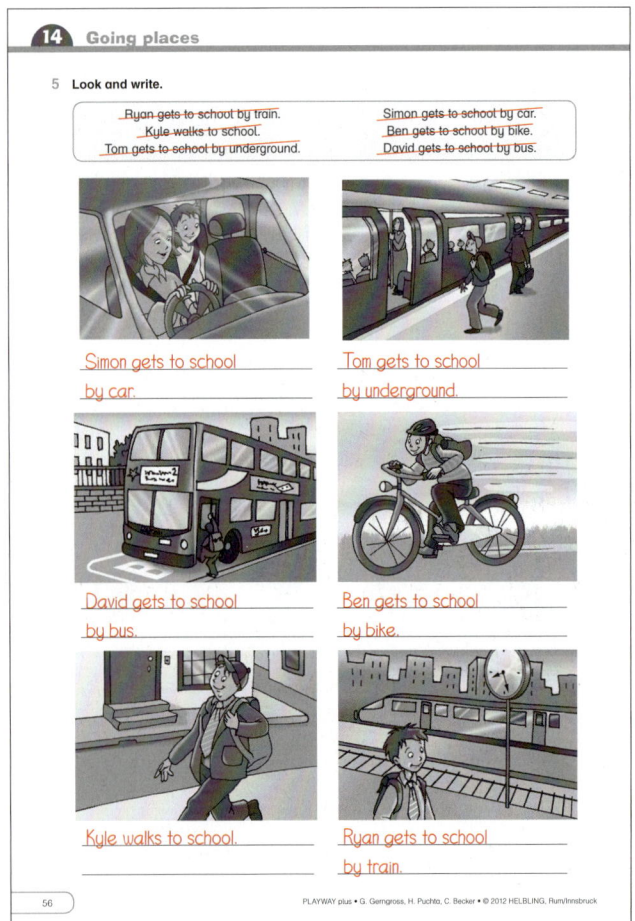

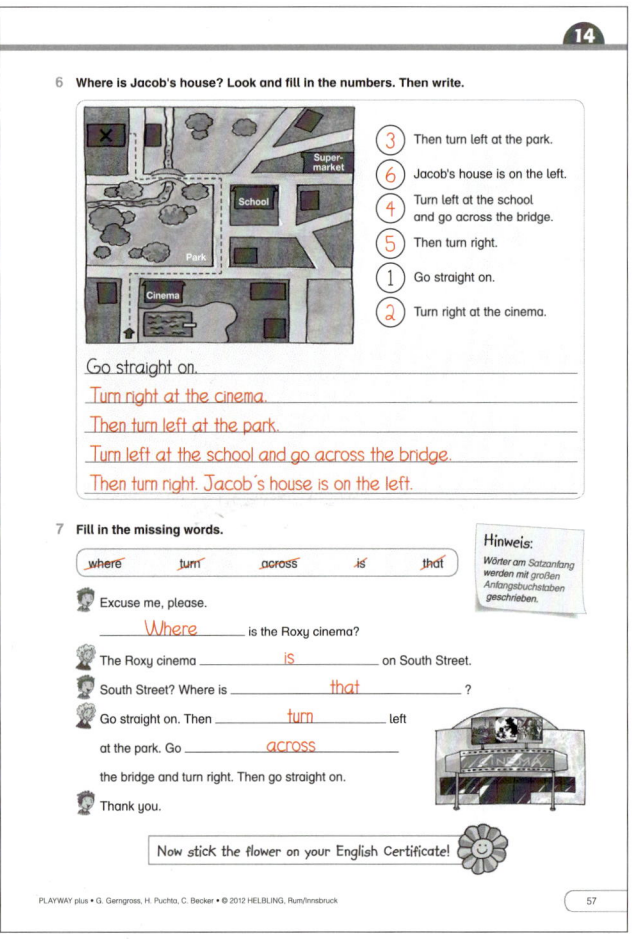

**14  Going places**

**1  Do the crossword.**

Across: 5 UNDERGROUND
1 BUS
BIKE, CAR, PLANE

**2  Look and write the names of the places.**

(1) school    (2) cinema    (3) zoo
(4) sweet shop    (5) supermarket

54

**14  Going places**

**3  Read and match.**

1 Excuse me, please. Where's the zoo? — 1 It's on Clifton Street.
2 Where's that? — 2 Go straight on. Turn right at the park.
3 Thank you. — 3 That's OK.
4 Bye, bye. — 4 Bye.

**4  Look and tick True or False (✓).**

Hinweis:
true = richtig
false = falsch

park    swimming pool    zoo
supermarket
cinema
sweet shop
school

| | True | False |
|---|---|---|
| The supermarket is next to the park. | ✓ | |
| The school is in front of the zoo. | | ✓ |
| The zoo is next to the swimming pool. | ✓ | |

| | True | False |
|---|---|---|
| The school is opposite the supermarket. | ✓ | |
| The bus stop is in front of the sweet shop. | ✓ | |
| The swimming pool is opposite the sweet shop. | | ✓ |

55

**14  Going places**

**5  Look and write.**

Ryan gets to school by train.    Simon gets to school by car.
Kyle walks to school.    Ben gets to school by bike.
Tom gets to school by underground.    David gets to school by bus.

Simon gets to school by car.    Tom gets to school by underground.

David gets to school by bus.    Ben gets to school by bike.

Kyle walks to school.    Ryan gets to school by train.

56

**6  Where is Jacob's house? Look and fill in the numbers. Then write.**

Supermarket    School    Park    Cinema

3 Then turn left at the park.
6 Jacob's house is on the left.
4 Turn left at the school and go across the bridge.
5 Then turn right.
1 Go straight on.
2 Turn right at the cinema.

Go straight on.
Turn right at the cinema.
Then turn left at the park.
Turn left at the school and go across the bridge.
Then turn right. Jacob's house is on the left.

**7  Fill in the missing words.**

where    turn    across    is    that

Hinweis:
Wörter am Satzanfang werden mit großen Anfangsbuchstaben geschrieben.

Excuse me, please.
Where is the Roxy cinema?
The Roxy cinema is on South Street.
South Street? Where is that?
Go straight on. Then turn left at the park. Go across the bridge and turn right. Then go straight on.
Thank you.

Now stick the flower on your English Certificate!

57

**7**  **Read the text and draw.**

In Linda's room the desk is in front of the window with the yellow curtains. There is a green chair in front of the desk. On the desk there is a lamp. The bed is opposite the desk. The wardrobe is behind the door. There is a small table between the door and the window with the blue curtains. On the bed there is a teddy bear. The schoolbag is under the bed.

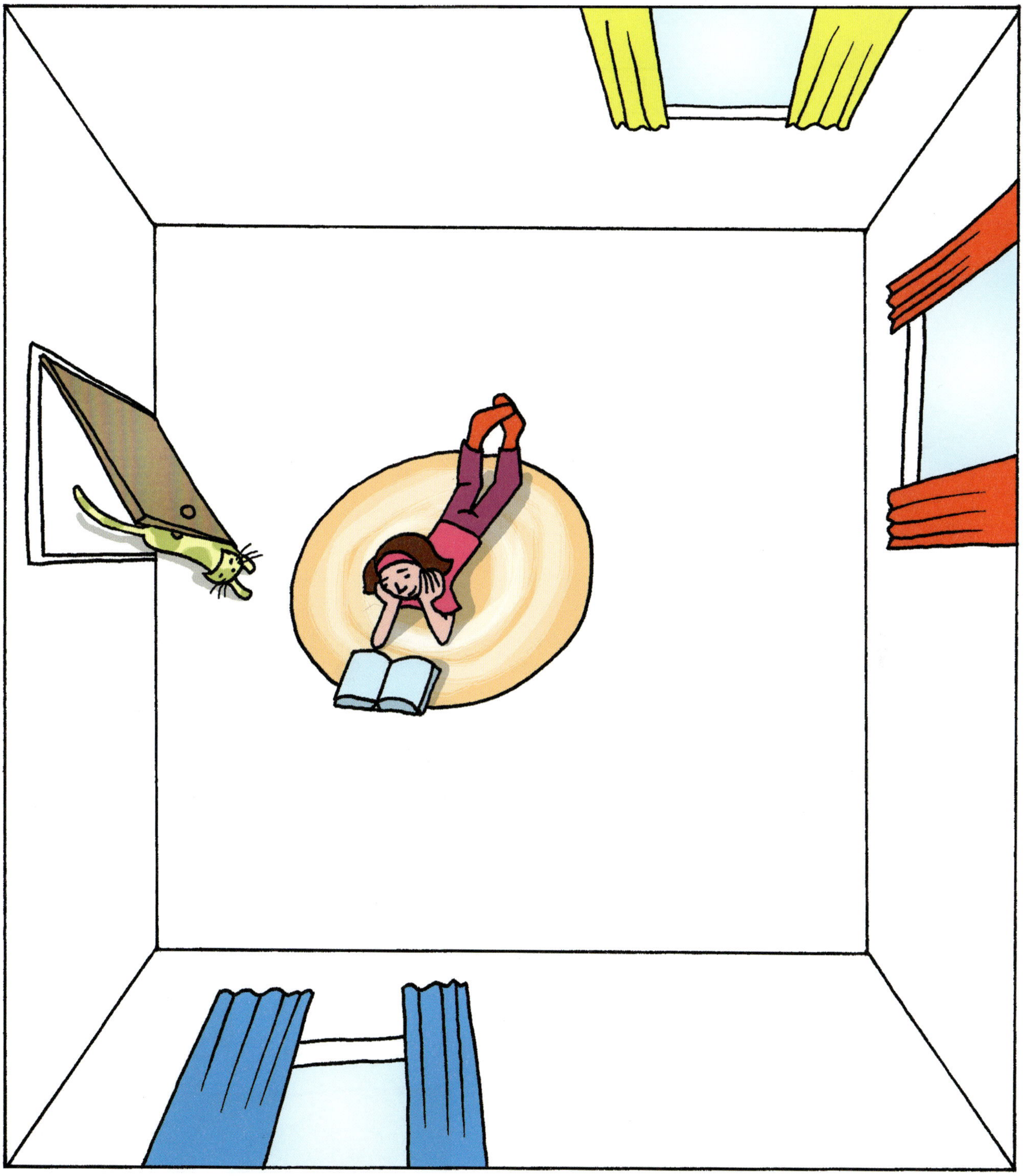

Now stick the flower on your English Certificate!

**1** **Write the words.**

① _____ : It is _____ .
(rain)                (rainy)

② _____ : It is _____ .
(clouds)              (cloudy)

③ _____ : It is _____ .
(sun)                (sunny)

④ _____ : It is _____ .
(wind)               (windy)

⑤ _____ : It is _____ .
(fog)                (foggy)

⑥ _____ : It is _____ .
(snow)               (snowy)

⑦ It is _____ .
(cold)

⑧ It is _____ .
(hot)

⑨ It is _____ .
(warm)

**2** **Complete.**

In winter, it is often cold_____ ,

f_____ and s_____ .

In spring, it is often su_____

and w_____ .

In summer, it is often very h_____ .

In autumn, it is often r_____ ,

w_____y and c_____ .

PLAYWAY plus • G. Gerngross, H. Puchta, C. Becker • © 2012 HELBLING, Rum/Innsbruck

**3** What's the weather like today? Look and complete.

JANUARY 12
1
MOSCOW    -15°C

JUNE 26
2
LONDON    23°C

JULY 30
3
PARIS    22°C

AUGUST 21
4
VIENNA    31°C

OCTOBER 18
5
NEW YORK    10°C

DECEMBER 9
6
SAN FRANCISCO    12°C

1  JANUARY **12**  What's the weather like today in Moscow?
It's snowy and cold. _____

2  JUNE **26**  What's the weather _____ in London?
It's _____ and _____ .

3  JULY **30**  _____ Paris?
_____ .

4  AUGUST **21**  _____ ?
_____ .

5  OCTOBER **18**  _____ ?
_____ .

6  DECEMBER **9**  _____ ?
_____ .

**4** **Read and write the names of the children under the photos.**

Hello, I'm David. I'm from Brighton in England.

It is often foggy and rainy here in winter. I don't like winter. Can you find my photo?

Hi, I'm Emily from Cape Town in South Africa.

In South Africa it is summer when it is winter in England. In our summer the weather is very nice. It's sunny and warm. Can you find my photo?

Hi, I'm Chuck, and I'm from Canada.

I live in Banff. There is a lot of snow in winter. I love it! Can you find my photo?

Hello, I'm Priya, and I live in India.

In the summer it's very, very hot, and it rains a lot. Then there is water on the streets. Can you find my photo?

_____

_____

_____

_____

PLAYWAY plus • G. Gerngross, H. Puchta, C. Becker • © 2012 HELBLING, Rum/Innsbruck

**5** **Match. Write the numbers.**

① What's the weather like today?

② It's cold. Where's my jacket?

③ It's hot. What would you like to drink?

④ That's a nice T-shirt. Can I try it on?

⑤ How many woolly hats have you got?

⑥ It's raining.

⑦ Who is the boy with the red pullover?

◯ Look. It's under the chair.

◯ It's Julian. My brother.

◯ I don't know. I think I have six.

◯ It's sunny and warm.

◯ Where's my umbrella?

◯ An orange juice, please.

◯ Yes, of course. That pullover is nice, too.

**6** **Fill in the missing words.**

how many   what   can   who   how   what   can   where

**Hinweis:**
Wörter am *Satzanfang* werden mit *großen Anfangsbuchstaben* geschrieben.

① _____ I help you? – Oh, yes, please. Thanks so much.

② _____ T-shirts have you got? – Ten, I think.

③ _____'s your brother? – He's at school.

④ _____'s your favourite food? – Fish and chips.

⑤ _____'s your favourite singer? – Sarah Green.

⑥ _____ would you like to eat? – A mixed salad, please.

⑦ _____ are you, Lucy? – I'm fine, thanks.

⑧ _____ you give me your book? – Yes, of course. Here you are.

Now stick the flower on your English Certificate!

**1**  **Look and write the words.**

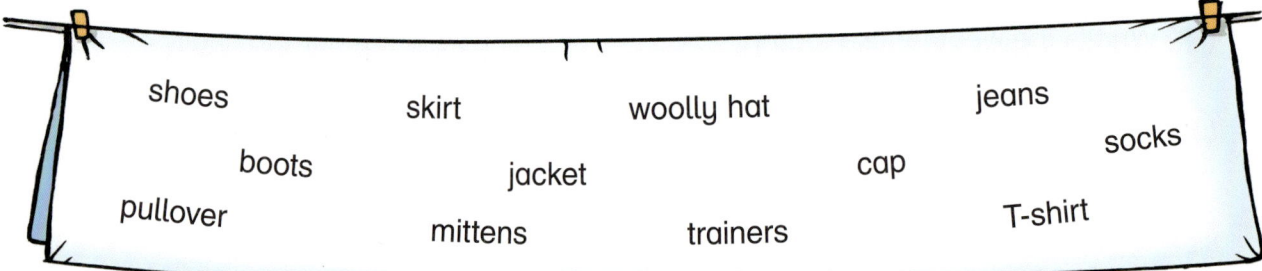

shoes          skirt          woolly hat          jeans

boots          jacket          cap          socks

pullover          mittens          trainers          T-shirt

_____    _____          _____          _____

_____

_____          _____          _____

_____

_____          _____          _____

PLAYWAY plus • G. Gerngross, H. Puchta, C. Becker • © 2012 HELBLING, Rum/Innsbruck

**2** **Read. Then colour the caps.**

This is John.
**His** cap is blue.

This is Anne.
**Her** cap is green.

**3** **Read and circle *His* or *Her*.**

1

*His / Her* favourite T-shirt
is from New York.

2

*His / Her* favourite T-shirt
is from Vienna.

3

*His / Her* favourite T-shirt
is from London.

4

*His / Her* favourite T-shirt
is from Berlin.

**4** **Read. Look at the pictures and fill in the numbers.**

1 Where's my cap?     2 Can I try it on?

3 Put on your jacket.     4 Take off your hat.

I'm hot.

It's on the cupboard.

I'm cold.

That T-shirt is nice.

**5** Write the names.

Mary     Larry     Carol     Ken

1. He is wearing blue jeans, a black T-shirt, a red cap and green trainers. Who is it?

   It's _____ .

2. He is wearing a black T-shirt, a red cap, blue jeans and white trainers. Who is it?

   It's _____ .

3. She is wearing blue jeans, a red cap, a pink T-shirt and green trainers. Who is it?

   It's _____ .

4. She is wearing green trainers, a red cap, black jeans and a pink T-shirt. Who is it?

   It's _____ .

**6** Look and write what Simon and Julia are wearing.

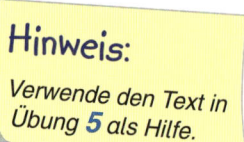

Hinweis:
Verwende den Text in Übung **5** als Hilfe.

1. Simon is wearing _____

   _____

   _____

   _____

2. Julia _____

   _____

   _____

   _____

Simon     Julia

PLAYWAY plus • G. Gerngross, H. Puchta, C. Becker • © 2012 HELBLING, Rum/Innsbruck

**7 Read and colour.**

Hinweis:
his cap → her cap

Benny's favourite T-shirt is red.
There's a big crocodile on it.
It's green.

His favourite cap is blue.
There's a yellow star on it.

**8 Look and write.**

Linda's favourite

Hinweis:
Verwende den Text in
Übung **7** als Hilfe.

Now stick the flower on your English Certificate!

PLAYWAY plus • G. Gerngross, H. Puchta, C. Becker • © 2012 HELBLING, Rum/Innsbruck

**1    Look, count and write. Then write the names.**

Hinweis:

*Zähle zuerst, wie viel Geld jeder hat.*
*Beantworte dann die Fragen darunter.*

Olivia: _____£ 7.45_____    Lucas: £ _____    Jacob: £ _____

Patrick: £ _____    Evelyn: £ _____    Norah: £ _____

1  Who has got fifty-seven pounds and fifty-five pence? _____

2  Who has got forty-three pounds? _____

3  Who has got fifteen pounds and ten pence? _____

4  Who has got forty-one pounds and sixty pence? _____

5  Who has got seven pounds and forty-five pence? _____

6  Who has got a hundred pounds? _____

**2    Circle the correct number.**

| thirty-three | (33) / 73 | thirteen | 13 / 30 | seventy | 17 / 70 |
|---|---|---|---|---|---|
| fourteen | 14 / 40 | seventy-one | 17 / 71 | forty-four | 34 / 44 |
| ninety-five | 59 / 95 | thirty-four | 34 / 24 | seventy-eight | 78 / 87 |

PLAYWAY plus • G. Gerngross, H. Puchta, C. Becker • © 2012 HELBLING, Rum/Innsbruck

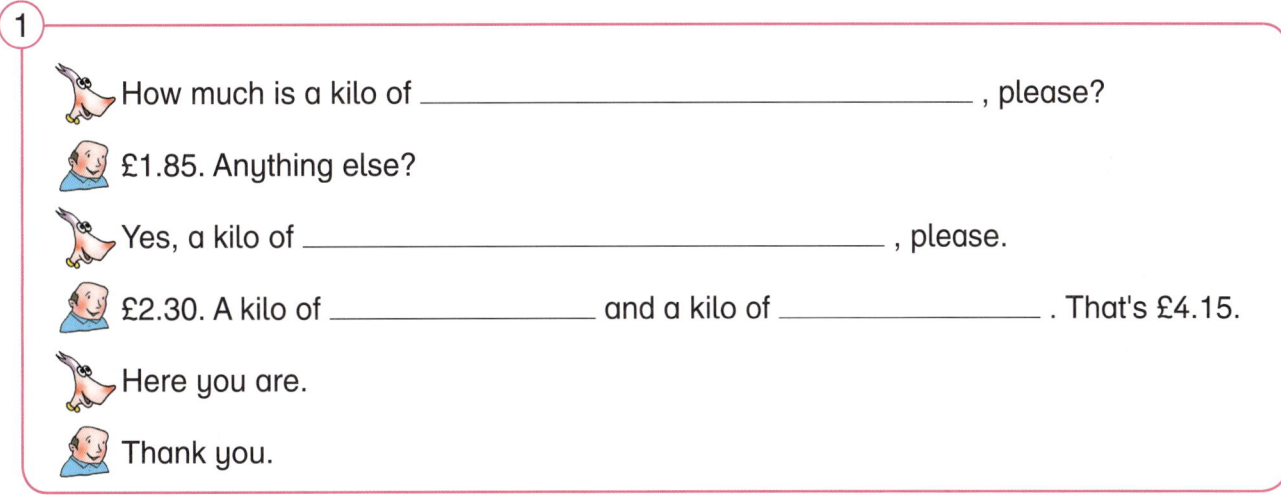

**3** Write the prices (p or £) for a kilo.

| | |
|---|---|
| carrots: | one pound twenty |
| onions: | ninety-five pence |
| cucumbers: | two pounds forty |
| peppers: | two pounds fifty |
| potatoes: | one pound eighty-five |
| tomatoes: | two pounds sixty |
| pears: | two pounds forty |
| apples: | one pound sixty-five |
| oranges: | two pounds thirty |
| plums: | one pound fifteen |
| bananas: | seventy-five pence |

**Hinweis:**
p = pence
£ = pound(s)
100 pence = 1 pound

_____ /kg

_____ /kg

_____ /kg

_____ /kg

_____ /kg

95p /kg

_____ /kg

_____ /kg

_____ /kg

_____ /kg

£1.20 /kg

**4** Look at the prices in **3**. Complete the dialogues.

**1**

How much is a kilo of _____ , please?

£1.85. Anything else?

Yes, a kilo of _____ , please.

£2.30. A kilo of _____ and a kilo of _____ . That's £4.15.

Here you are.

Thank you.

**2**

How much is a kilo of _____ pears, please?

_____ . _____ ?

Yes, _____ carrots, _____ .

£1.20. A kilo of _____ and a kilo of _____ . _____ .

_____ .

_____ .

## 5 Read and write.

> Yes, it's very good.
> Sorry, Mum, I'm busy.
>
> Chicken and vegetables.
> I forgot the milk.

PLAYWAY plus • G. Gerngross, H. Puchta, C. Becker • © 2012 HELBLING, Rum/Innsbruck

**6** **Circle _is_ or _are_.**

(1) How much _is / are_ the DVDs?  £10.85

(2) How much _is / are_ the green bike?  £85

(3) How much _is / are_ the blue cap?  £6.99

(4) How much _is / are_ the jeans?  £45.40

(5) How much _is / are_ the books?  £12.50

(6) How much _is / are_ the shoes?  £19.50

Hinweis:

_How much is …?_ verwendest du für die Einzahl, z. B.: _How much is the pencil?_

_How much are …?_ verwendest du für die Mehrzahl, z. B.: _How much are the pencils?_

Achtung: "jeans" ist ein Mehrzahlwort

**7** **Read and tick the correct picture. (✔)**

Samuel often goes shopping for his mum. He buys fruit, eggs and milk.
He also buys bread, butter and cheese.

  ☐      ☐

**8** **Look and write what Lilly buys for her mum.**

Hinweis:

Verwende den Text in Übung **7** als Hilfe.

Lilly _____

_____ .

_____ vegetables

and e_____ .

_____

br_____ and

ch_____ .

Now stick the flower on your English Certificate!

## 12  Free time

**1**  **Do the crossword.**

1. P L A Y ▮ F O O T B A L L

PLAYWAY plus • G. Gerngross, H. Puchta, C. Becker • © 2012 HELBLING, Rum/Innsbruck

**2** Write what Leah does.

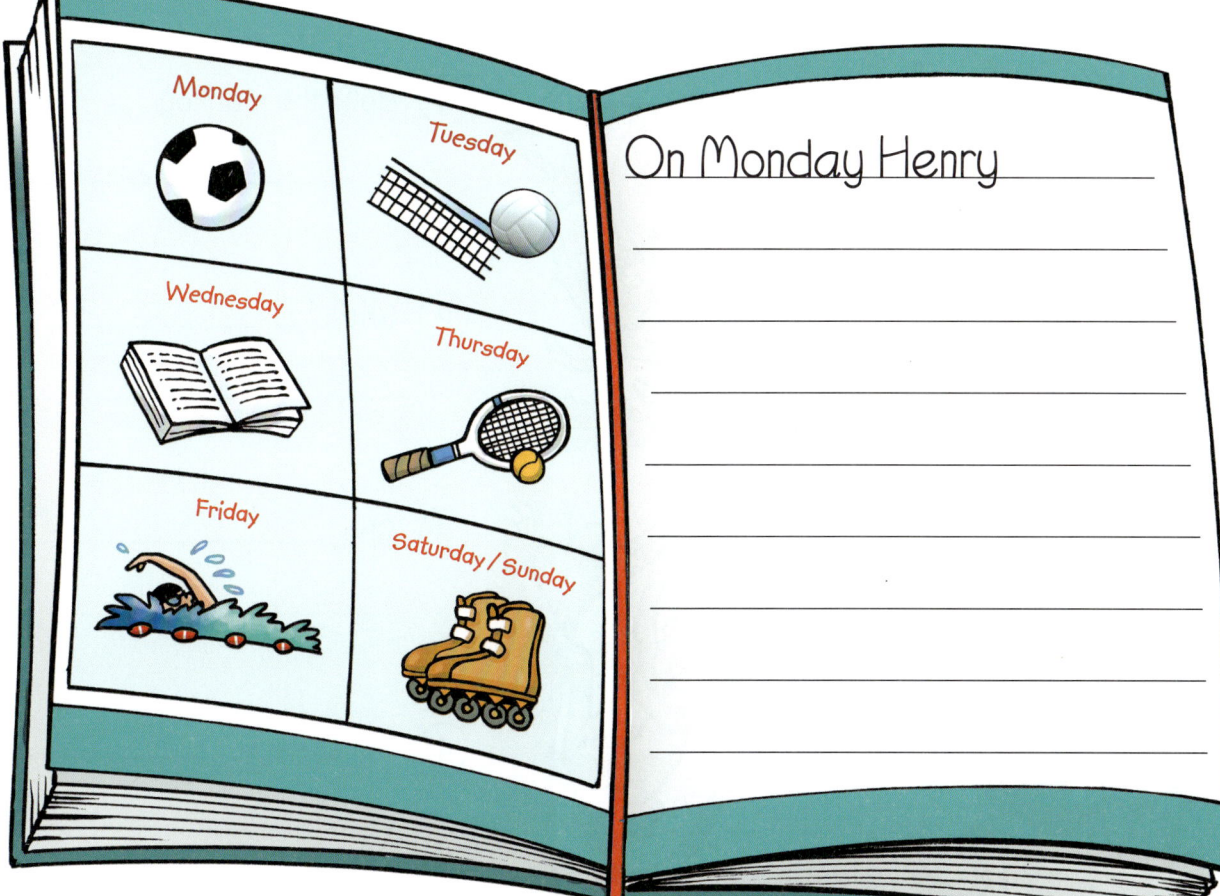

On Monday Leah listens to music.

On Tuesday she goes shopping.

On <u>Wednesday she goes in-line skating</u> .

On _____

her _____ .

On _____ .

On Saturday and Sunday _____

_____ her _____ .

**3** Write what Henry does.

<u>On Monday Henry</u> _____

_____

_____

_____

_____

_____

_____

_____

**4** Write about Swimmy the crocodile.

1 Swimmy the crocodile can't climb a _____ .

2 He can't _____ _____ .

3 He _____ _____ .

4 But he can _____ _____ .

**5** Write about Bella the monkey.

1 Bella the monkey _____ _____ .

2 She _____ _____ .

3 She _____ _____ .

4 But she _____ _____ .

PLAYWAY plus • G. Gerngross, H. Puchta, C. Becker • © 2012 HELBLING, Rum/Innsbruck

**6** **Look at the pictures and complete the dialogues.**

| Yes, I can. | Can you | No, I can't. | Can you |

*Vicky:* _____ ride a horse?          *Vicky:* _____ ride a unicycle?

*Julia:* _____          *Julia:* _____

**7** **Look and write the dialogues.**

*Ryan:* _____ ?          *Ryan:* _____ ?

*Luke:* _____          *Luke:* _____

Now stick the flower on your English Certificate!

**1**  **What's the time? Read and match.**

◯ It's eleven o'clock.

◯ It's half past three.

◯ It's half past ten.

◯ It's two o'clock.

◯ It's quarter past midnight.

◯ It's quarter past nine.

◯ It's quarter to eleven.

◯ It's quarter to seven.

PLAYWAY plus • G. Gerngross, H. Puchta, C. Becker • © 2012 HELBLING, Rum/Innsbruck

**2  Read and draw.**

It's six o'clock.   It's half past four.   It's quarter to five.   It's half past five.

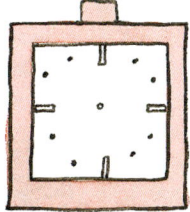    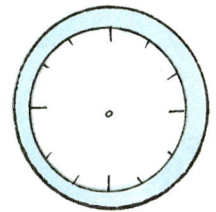  

It's quarter past nine.   It's three o'clock.   It's quarter past one.   It's quarter to two.

**3  Look at the pictures. Complete the sentences.**

1     2     3

4     5     6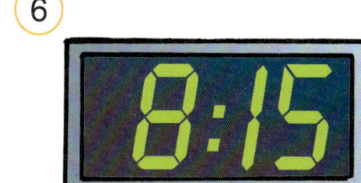

1  It's _____ .
2  It's _____ .
3  It's _____ .
4  It's _____ .
5  It's _____ .
6  It's _____ .
7  It's _____ .
8  It's _____ .

7

8

**4** **Look. Match the pictures with the sentences.**

Linda goes to bed at nine o'clock.

She goes to school at half past eight.

Linda gets up at half past six.

She has breakfast at quarter past seven.

She comes home at three o'clock.

**5** **Look and write the answers.**

Hinweis:
Schreibe ganze Sätze.
Verwende den Text in
Übung 4 als Hilfe.

1 What time does Benny get up? <u>Benny gets up at</u> _____

2 What time does he have breakfast? <u>He</u> _____

3 What time does he go to school? _____

4 What time does he come home? _____

5 What time does he go to bed? _____

PLAYWAY plus • G. Gerngross, H. Puchta, C. Becker • © 2012 HELBLING, Rum/Innsbruck

**6** **Look and write.**

| play tennis | go to bed | go in-line skating | ~~get up~~ | read a book |

7:30    10:45    13:15    17:00    20:30

Alex and Mike get up at half past seven. _____

They _____

_____

_____

_____

**7** **Look and write.**

| sail a boat | ride my bike | ~~get up~~ | go to bed | play volleyball |

7:00    9:15    13:45    16:30    20:45

I get up at _____

_____

_____

_____

_____

Now stick the flower on your English Certificate!

**1** Do the crossword.

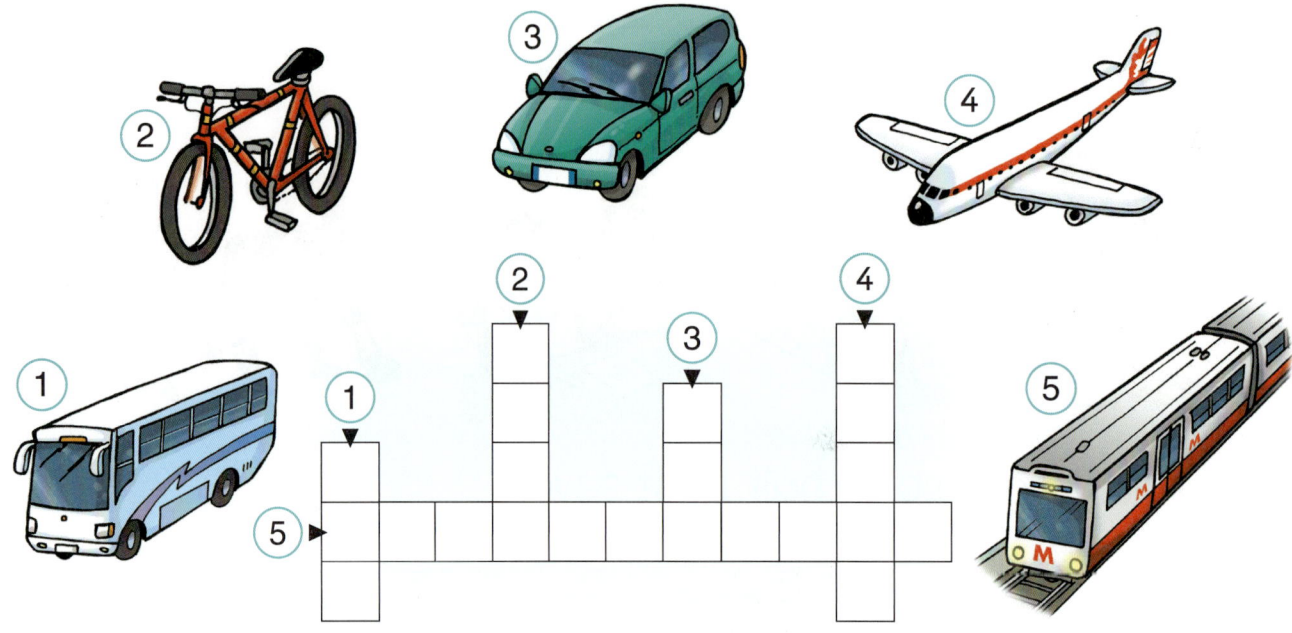

**2** Look and write the names of the places.

1 _____ school _____     2 _____     3 _____

4 _____     5 _____

PLAYWAY plus • G. Gerngross, H. Puchta, C. Becker • © 2012 HELBLING, Rum/Innsbruck

## 3  Read and match.

1  Excuse me, please. Where's the zoo?

2  Where's that?

3  Thank you.

4  Bye, bye.

◯  Bye.

◯  It's on Clifton Street.

◯  Go straight on. Turn right at the park.

◯  That's OK.

## 4  Look and tick *True* or *False* (✓).

Hinweis:
*true* = richtig
*false* = falsch

park

swimming pool

zoo

supermarket

cinema

sweet shop

school

|  | True | False |
|---|---|---|
| The supermarket is next to the park. | ☐ | ☐ |
| The school is in front of the zoo. | ☐ | ☐ |
| The zoo is next to the swimming pool. | ☐ | ☐ |

|  | True | False |
|---|---|---|
| The school is opposite the supermarket. | ☐ | ☐ |
| The bus stop is in front of the sweet shop. | ☐ | ☐ |
| The swimming pool is opposite the sweet shop. | ☐ | ☐ |

## 5 Look and write.

Ryan gets to school by train.
Kyle walks to school.
Tom gets to school by underground.

Simon gets to school by car.
Ben gets to school by bike.
David gets to school by bus.

_____

_____

_____

_____

_____

_____

PLAYWAY plus • G. Gerngross, H. Puchta, C. Becker • © 2012 HELBLING, Rum/Innsbruck

**6** **Where is Jacob's house? Look and fill in the numbers. Then write.**

○ Then turn left at the park.

○ Jacob's house is on the left.

○ Turn left at the school and go across the bridge.

○ Then turn right.

① Go straight on.

○ Turn right at the cinema.

Go straight on. _____

_____

_____

_____

_____

**7** **Fill in the missing words.**

| where | turn | across | is | that |

Hinweis:
Wörter am *Satzanfang* werden mit *großen Anfangsbuchstaben* geschrieben.

 Excuse me, please.

_____ is the Roxy cinema?

Image Description: The Roxy cinema _____ on South Street.

South Street? Where is _____ ?

Image Description: Go straight on. Then _____ left

at the park. Go _____

the bridge and turn right. Then go straight on.

Thank you.

Now stick the flower on your English Certificate!

## A

| | |
|---|---|
| a/an | ein/e |
| and | und |
| angry | wütend |
| animal | Tier |
| answer | Antwort; antworten |
| **Anything else?** | hier: Darf es noch etwas sein? |
| apple | Apfel |
| arm | Arm |
| attic | Dachboden |
| autumn | Herbst |

## B

| | |
|---|---|
| bag | Tasche, Beutel, Tüte |
| ball | Ball |
| banana | Banane |
| bathroom | Badezimmer |
| bean | Bohne |
| bed | Bett |
| bedroom | Schlafzimmer |
| bee | Biene |
| behind | hinter |
| **best friend** | beste/r Freund/in |
| big | groß |
| bike | Fahrrad |
| black | schwarz |
| blue | blau |
| board | Tafel |
| boat | Boot |
| body | Körper |
| book | Buch |
| boots | Stiefel |
| boy | Junge |
| bread | Brot |
| breakfast | Frühstück |
| brother | Bruder |
| brown | braun |
| budgie | Wellensittich |
| bus | Bus |
| **bus stop** | Bushaltestelle |
| busy | beschäftigt |
| but | aber |
| butter | Butter |
| butterfly | Schmetterling |
| buy | kaufen |

## C

| | |
|---|---|
| cake | Torte |
| can/can't | können/nicht können |
| Canada | Kanada |
| cap | Kappe |
| **Cape Town** | Kapstadt |
| car | Auto |
| careful | vorsichtig |
| carrot | Karotte |
| cat | Katze |
| certificate | Urkunde |
| chair | Stuhl |
| check | nachsehen, überprüfen |
| cheese | Käse |
| chicken | Hühnchen |
| child/children | Kind/Kinder |
| chips | Pommes frites |
| cinema | Kino |
| circle | einkreisen |
| clap | klatschen |
| **climb a tree** | auf einen Baum klettern |
| clothes | Kleidung |
| cloud | Wolke |
| cloudy | bewölkt |
| cola | Cola |
| cold | kalt |
| colour | Farbe; anmalen |
| **come home** | nach Hause kommen |

| | |
|---|---|
| complete | vervollständigen |
| cook | kochen |
| correct | richtig |
| count | zählen |
| crocodile | Krokodil |
| crossword | Kreuzworträtsel |
| cucumber | Salatgurke |
| cup | Tasse |
| cupboard | Schrank |
| curtains | Vorhänge |

## D

| | |
|---|---|
| dad | Papa |
| dance | tanzen |
| **Dear** (Julia/Peter) | Liebe/r (Julia/Peter) |
| desk | Schreibtisch |
| dessert | Nachspeise |
| dialogue | Dialog |
| **Do you like ...?** | Magst du ...? |
| do/does | machen |
| dog | Hund |
| **don't/doesn't like** | nicht mögen |
| door | Tür |
| draw | zeichnen |
| drink | trinken; Getränk |
| duck | Ente |

## E

| | |
|---|---|
| eat | essen |
| egg | Ei |
| **excuse me** | entschuldige/entschuldigen Sie |
| eye | Auge |

## F

| | |
|---|---|
| family | Familie |
| fast | schnell |
| favourite | Lieblings- |
| **I feel sick.** | Mir ist übel. |
| feeling | Gefühl |
| feet | Füße |
| **fill in** | einfüllen |
| find | finden |
| **I'm fine.** | Mir geht es gut. |
| finger | Finger |
| fish | Fisch |
| **fish and chips** | Fisch und Pommes frites |
| flower | Blume |
| fly | Fliege; fliegen |
| fog | Nebel |
| foggy | nebelig |
| food | Essen |
| (play) **football** | Fußball (spielen) |
| for | für |
| **forget** (Vergangenheit: **forgot**) | vergessen |
| fossil | Fossil |
| **free time** | Freizeit |
| Friday | Freitag |
| frog | Frosch |
| **from up there** | von dort oben |
| fruit | Obst |
| **fruit salad** | Obstsalat |

## G

| | |
|---|---|
| I **get to school** by bus. | Ich komme mit dem Bus zur Schule. |
| **get up** | aufstehen |
| girl | Mädchen |
| go | gehen |
| **go out** | hinausgehen |
| **go shopping** | einkaufen gehen |
| **go straight on** | geradeaus gehen |
| **go to bed/school** | zu Bett/in die Schule gehen |

PLAYWAY plus • G. Gerngross, H. Puchta, C. Becker • © 2012 HELBLING, Rum/Innsbruck

| | |
|---|---|
| grandma | Großmutter |
| grandpa | Großvater |
| grass | Gras |
| great | großartig |
| green | grün |
| grey | grau |

**H**

| | |
|---|---|
| hair | Haare |
| half past (three) | halb (vier) |
| hall | Flur |
| ham | Schinken |
| hamburger | Hamburger |
| happy | glücklich |
| have a glass of milk | ein Glas Milch trinken |
| have breakfast | frühstücken |
| have got/has got | haben/hat |
| he | er |
| head | Kopf |
| her | ihr/e |
| here | hier |
| Here you are. | Bitte sehr. |
| his | sein/e |
| at **home** | zu Hause |
| horse | Pferd |
| hot | heiß |
| how | wie |
| how many | wie viel/wie viele |
| how much | wie viel |
| hungry | hungrig |
| hurt | schmerzen |

**I**

| | |
|---|---|
| I | ich |
| ice cream | Eiscreme |
| I'd like/I would like … | Ich hätte gerne … |
| I'm having steak. | hier: Ich nehme ein Steak. |
| in | in |
| in front of | vor |
| India | Indien |
| in-line skate | inlineskaten |
| interesting | interessant |
| it | es |
| It's … o'clock. | Es ist … Uhr. |

**J**

| | |
|---|---|
| jacket | Jacke |
| jeans | Jeans |

**K**

| | |
|---|---|
| ketchup | Ketchup |
| kilo | Kilo(gramm) |
| kitchen | Küche |
| knee | Knie |
| know | wissen |

**L**

| | |
|---|---|
| lamp | Lampe |
| lay eggs | Eier legen |
| left | links |
| leg | Bein |
| lemonade | Limonade |
| Let's go. | Lass uns gehen./Gehen wir. |
| like | mögen |
| lion | Löwe |
| listen (to) | (zu)hören |
| living room | Wohnzimmer |
| look at | ansehen, anschauen |
| a **lot of/lots of** | viel/e |
| love | lieben |

**M**

| | |
|---|---|
| match | zuordnen |

| | |
|---|---|
| me | mir/mich |
| menu | Speisekarte |
| midnight | Mitternacht |
| milk | Milch |
| mineral water | Mineralwasser |
| missing | fehlend/e |
| mittens | Fäustlinge |
| mixed salad | gemischter Salat |
| **Monday** | Montag |
| monkey | Affe |
| mouth | Mund |
| mum | Mama |
| museum | Museum |
| music | Musik |
| my | mein/e |

**N**

| | |
|---|---|
| name | Name |
| **Natural History Museum** | Naturgeschichtliches Museum |
| new | neu |
| next to | neben |
| nice | nett, schön; auch: gut |
| no | nein |
| nose | Nase |
| number | Zahl |

**O**

| | |
|---|---|
| of course | natürlich |
| often | oft |
| old | alt |
| on | auf |
| onion | Zwiebel |
| opposite | gegenüber |
| or | oder |
| orange | orange; Orange |
| orange juice | Orangensaft |
| other | andere/r/s |
| Ouch! | Aua! |
| our | unser/e |

**P**

| | |
|---|---|
| park | Park |
| pear | Birne |
| peas | Erbsen |
| pen | Kugelschreiber |
| pence | Pence (britisches Geld) |
| pencil | Bleistift |
| pepper | Paprika |
| picture | Bild |
| pink | pink |
| pizza | Pizza |
| place | Ort |
| plane | Flugzeug |
| play | spielen |
| please | bitte |
| plum | Pflaume |
| pony | Pony |
| potato | Kartoffel |
| pound | Pfund (britische Währung) |
| price | Preis |
| pullover | Pullover |
| put in | hineingeben |
| put on | anziehen |

**Q**

| | |
|---|---|
| quarter past (nine) | viertel nach (neun) |
| quarter to (eleven) | viertel vor (elf) |

**R**

| | |
|---|---|
| rabbit | Hase |
| rain | Regen |
| rainy | regnerisch |
| read (a book) | (ein Buch) lesen |

| | | | |
|---|---|---|---|
| red | rot | teddy bear | Teddybär |
| restaurant | Restaurant | (play) **tennis** | Tennis (spielen) |
| rice | Reis | **Thanks./Thank you.** | Danke. |
| ride a bike/unicycle | Fahrrad/Einrad fahren | the | der/die/das |
| ride a horse | reiten | then | danach |
| right | rechts | **There is/There are …** | Es gibt … |
| room | Zimmer | they | sie (Mehrzahl) |
| rubber | Radiergummi | think | denken |
| ruler | Lineal | **Thursday** | Donnerstag |
| run | rennen | tick | anhaken |
| | | time | Zeit |

**S**

| | | | |
|---|---|---|---|
| sad | traurig | tired | müde |
| sail a boat | segeln | toast | Toast |
| sandwich | Sandwich | today | heute |
| **Saturday** | Samstag | toe(s) | Zeh(en) |
| sausages | Würstchen | tomato | Tomate |
| scared | verängstigt | too | auch |
| school | Schule | tooth/teeth | Zahn/Zähne |
| schoolbag | Schultasche | touch | berühren |
| scissors | Schere | trainers | Turnschuhe |
| season | Jahreszeit | try on | anprobieren |
| see | sehen | **T-shirt** | T-Shirt |
| sentence | Satz | **Tuesday** | Dienstag |
| shake | schütteln | turn right/left | rechts/links abbiegen |
| she | sie | | |

**U**

| | | | |
|---|---|---|---|
| sheep | Schaf | umbrella | Schirm |
| shoes | Schuhe | under | unter |
| shoulder | Schulter | underground | U-Bahn |
| sing (a song) | (ein Lied) singen | unicycle | Einrad |
| sister | Schwester | use | verwenden |

| | | | |
|---|---|---|---|
| skate | eislaufen | | |
| skateboard | Skateboard | **V** | |
| ski | Schi fahren | vegetables | Gemüse |
| skirt | Rock | very | sehr |
| small | klein | **Vienna** | Wien |
| snake | Schlange | (play) **volleyball** | Volleyball (spielen) |
| snow | Schnee | | |
| snowboard | snowboarden | **W** | |
| snowy | verschneit | | |
| **So am I.** | Ich auch. | walk to school | zu Fuß zur Schule gehen |
| socks | Socken | wardrobe | Kleiderschrank |
| sofa | Sofa | warm | warm |
| soon | bald | watch | Armbanduhr |
| I'm **sorry.** | Es tut mir leid. | we | wir |
| **South Africa** | Südafrika | wear | Kleidung tragen |
| spaghetti | Spaghetti | weather | Wetter |
| spinach | Spinat | **Wednesday** | Mittwoch |
| spring | Frühling | what | was |
| stairs | Treppe(n) | where | wo |
| star | Stern | white | weiß |
| start | anfangen | who | wer |
| steak | Steak | wind | Wind |
| stick (in) | einkleben | window | Fenster |
| story | Geschichte | windy | windig |
| strawberry | Erdbeere | winter | Winter |
| street | Straße | with | mit |
| sugar | Zucker | woolly hat | Wollmütze |
| summer | Sommer | word | Wort |
| sun | Sonne | **Would you like …?** | Möchten Sie/Möchtest du …? |
| **Sunday** | Sonntag | write (about) | schreiben (über) |
| sunny | sonnig | | |
| supermarket | Supermarkt | **Y** | |
| sweet shop | Süßwarengeschäft | | |
| swim | schwimmen | year | Jahr |
| swimming pool | Schwimmbad | yellow | gelb |
| | | yes | ja |
| | | you | du; ihr |
| **T** | | your | dein/e; euer/eure |
| table | Tisch | | |
| take | nehmen | **Z** | |
| take off | Kleidung ausziehen | | |
| tea | Tee | zoo | Zoo |
| teacher | Lehrer/in | | |

PLAYWAY plus • G. Gerngross, H. Puchta, C. Becker • © 2012 HELBLING, Rum/Innsbruck

### A

| | |
|---|---|
| aber | but |
| Affe | monkey |
| alt | old |
| andere/r/s | other |
| anfangen | start |
| anhaken | tick |
| anmalen | colour |
| anprobieren | try on |
| ansehen | look at |
| Antwort; antworten | answer |
| anziehen | put on |
| Apfel | apple |
| Arm | arm |
| Armbanduhr | watch |
| Aua! | Ouch! |
| auch | too |
| auf | on |
| aufstehen | get up |
| Auge | eye |
| Kleidung ausziehen | take off |
| Auto | car |

### B

| | |
|---|---|
| Badezimmer | bathroom |
| bald | soon |
| Ball | ball |
| Banane | banana |
| Bein | leg |
| berühren | touch |
| beschäftigt | busy |
| beste/r Freund/in | best friend |
| Bett | bed |
| bewölkt | cloudy |
| Biene | bee |
| Bild | picture |
| Birne | pear |
| bitte | please |
| Bitte sehr./Da hast du es. | Here you are. |
| blau | blue |
| Bleistift | pencil |
| Blume | flower |
| Bohne | bean |
| Boot | boat |
| braun | brown |
| Brot | bread |
| Bruder | brother |
| Buch | book |
| Bus | bus |
| Bushaltestelle | bus stop |
| Butter | butter |

### C

| | |
|---|---|
| Cola | cola |

### D

| | |
|---|---|
| Dachboden | attic |
| danach | then |
| Danke. | Thanks./Thank you. |
| Darf es noch etwas sein? | Anything else? |
| dein/e | your |
| denken | think |
| der/die/das | the |
| Dialog | dialogue |
| Dienstag | Tuesday |
| Donnerstag | Thursday |
| du | you |

### E

| | |
|---|---|
| Ei | egg |
| Eier legen | lay eggs |
| ein/e | a/an |
| einfüllen | fill in |
| einkaufen gehen | go shopping |

| | |
|---|---|
| einkleben | stick (in) |
| einkreisen | circle |
| Einrad | unicycle |
| Eiscreme | ice cream |
| eislaufen | skate |
| Ente | duck |
| entschuldige/ entschuldigen Sie | excuse me |
| er | he |
| Erbsen | peas |
| Erdbeere | strawberry |
| es | it |
| Es gibt … | There is/There are … |
| Es ist … Uhr. | It's … o'clock. |
| Es tut mir leid. | I'm sorry. |
| essen | eat |
| Essen | food |
| euer/eure | your |

### F

| | |
|---|---|
| Fahrrad | bike |
| Fahrrad/Einrad fahren | ride a bike/unicycle |
| Familie | family |
| Farbe | colour |
| Fäustlinge | mittens |
| fehlend/e | missing |
| Fenster | window |
| finden | find |
| Finger | finger |
| Fisch | fish |
| Fisch und Pommes frites | fish and chips |
| Fliege; fliegen | fly |
| Flugzeug | plane |
| Flur | hall |
| Fossil | fossil |
| Freitag | Friday |
| Freizeit | free time |
| Frosch | frog |
| Frühling | spring |
| Frühstück | breakfast |
| frühstücken | have breakfast |
| für | for |
| Füße | feet |
| Fußball (spielen) | (play) football |

### G

| | |
|---|---|
| Gefühl | feeling |
| gegenüber | opposite |
| gehen | go |
| zu Bett/in die Schule gehen | go to bed/school |
| zu Fuß zur Schule gehen | walk to school |
| gelb | yellow |
| gemischter Salat | mixed salad |
| Gemüse | vegetables |
| geradeaus gehen | go straight on |
| Geschichte | story |
| Getränk | drink |
| ein Glas Milch trinken | have a glass of milk |
| glücklich | happy |
| Gras | grass |
| grau | grey |
| groß | big |
| großartig | great |
| Großmutter | grandma |
| Großvater | grandpa |
| grün | green |
| Mir geht es gut. | I'm fine. |

### H

| | |
|---|---|
| Haare | hair |
| haben/hat | have got/has got |
| halb (vier) | half past (three) |
| Hamburger | hamburger |

| | | |
|---|---|---|
| Hase |  | rabbit |
| heiß | | hot |
| Herbst | | autumn |
| heute | | today |
| hier | | here |
| hinausgehen | | go out |
| hineingeben | | put in |
| hinter | | behind |
| (zu)hören | | listen (to) |
| Hühnchen | | chicken |
| Hund | | dog |
| hungrig | | hungry |

**I**

| | |
|---|---|
| ich | I |
| Ich hätte gerne … | I'd like/I would like … |
| ihr (Mehrzahl) | you |
| ihr/e | her |
| in | in |
| Indien | India |
| inlineskaten | in-line skate |
| interessant | interesting |

**J**

| | |
|---|---|
| ja | yes |
| Jacke | jacket |
| Jahr | year |
| Jahreszeit | season |
| Jeans | jeans |
| Junge | boy |

**K**

| | |
|---|---|
| kalt | cold |
| Kanada | Canada |
| Kappe | cap |
| Kapstadt | Cape Town |
| Karotte | carrot |
| Kartoffel | potato |
| Käse | cheese |
| Katze | cat |
| kaufen | buy |
| Ketchup | ketchup |
| Kilo(gramm) | kilo |
| Kind/Kinder | child/children |
| Kino | cinema |
| klatschen | clap |
| Kleiderschrank | wardrobe |
| Kleidung | clothes |
| klein | small |
| auf einen Baum klettern | climb a tree |
| Knie | knee |
| kochen | cook |
| Ich komme mit dem Bus zur Schule. | I get to school by bus. |
| nach Hause kommen | come home |
| können/nicht können | can/can't |
| Kopf | head |
| Körper | body |
| Kreuzworträtsel | crossword |
| Krokodil | crocodile |
| Küche | kitchen |
| Kugelschreiber | pen |

**L**

| | |
|---|---|
| Lampe | lamp |
| Lass uns gehen./Gehen wir. | Let's go. |
| Lehrer/in | teacher |
| (ein Buch) lesen | read (a book) |
| Liebe/r (Julia/Peter) | Dear (Julia/Peter) |
| lieben | love |
| Lieblings- | favourite |
| Limonade | lemonade |
| Lineal | ruler |

| | | |
|---|---|---|
| links (abbiegen) |  | (turn) left |
| Löwe | | lion |

**M**

| | |
|---|---|
| machen | do/does |
| Mädchen | girl |
| Magst du …? | Do you like …? |
| Mama | mum |
| mein/e | my |
| mich | me |
| Milch | milk |
| Mineralwasser | mineral water |
| mir | me |
| mit | with |
| Mitternacht | midnight |
| Mittwoch | Wednesday |
| Möchten Sie/Möchtest du …? | Would you like …? |
| mögen | like |
| Montag | Monday |
| müde | tired |
| Mund | mouth |
| Museum | museum |
| Musik | music |

**N**

| | |
|---|---|
| nachsehen | check |
| Nachspeise | dessert |
| Name | name |
| Nase | nose |
| Naturgeschichtliches Museum | Natural History Museum |
| natürlich | of course |
| Nebel | fog |
| nebelig | foggy |
| neben | next to |
| nehmen | take |
| nein | no |
| nett | nice |
| neu | new |
| nicht mögen | don't/doesn't like |

**O**

| | |
|---|---|
| Obst | fruit |
| Obstsalat | fruit salad |
| oder | or |
| oft | often |
| orange; Orange | orange |
| Orangensaft | orange juice |
| Ort | place |

**P**

| | |
|---|---|
| Papa | dad |
| Paprika | pepper |
| Park | park |
| Pence (britisches Geld) | pence |
| Pferd | horse |
| Pflaume | plum |
| Pfund (britische Währung) | pound |
| pink | pink |
| Pizza | pizza |
| Pommes frites | chips |
| Pony | pony |
| Preis | price |
| Pullover | pullover |

**R**

| | |
|---|---|
| Radiergummi | rubber |
| rechts (abbiegen) | (turn) right |
| Regen | rain |
| regnerisch | rainy |
| Reis | rice |
| reiten | ride a horse |
| rennen | run |
| Restaurant | restaurant |

PLAYWAY plus • G. Gerngross, H. Puchta, C. Becker • © 2012 HELBLING, Rum/Innsbruck

| | |
|---|---|
| **richtig** | correct |
| **Rock** | skirt |
| **rot** | red |

### S

| | |
|---|---|
| **Salatgurke** | cucumber |
| **Samstag** | Saturday |
| **Sandwich** | sandwich |
| **Satz** | sentence |
| **Schaf** | sheep |
| **Schere** | scissors |
| **Schi fahren** | ski |
| **Schinken** | ham |
| **Schirm** | umbrella |
| **Schlafzimmer** | bedroom |
| **Schlange** | snake |
| **schmerzen** | hurt |
| **Schmetterling** | butterfly |
| **Schnee** | snow |
| **schnell** | fast |
| **Schrank** | cupboard |
| **schreiben (über)** | write (about) |
| **Schreibtisch** | desk |
| **Schuhe** | shoes |
| **Schule** | school |
| **Schultasche** | schoolbag |
| **Schulter** | shoulder |
| **schütteln** | shake |
| **schwarz** | black |
| **Schwester** | sister |
| **Schwimmbad** | swimming pool |
| **schwimmen** | swim |
| **segeln** | sail a boat |
| **sehen** | see |
| **sehr** | very |
| **sein/e** | his |
| **sie** | she; they |
| **singen** | sing (a song) |
| **Skateboard** | skateboard |
| **snowboarden** | snowboard |
| **Socken** | socks |
| **Sofa** | sofa |
| **Sommer** | summer |
| **Sonne** | sun |
| **sonnig** | sunny |
| **Sonntag** | Sunday |
| **Spaghetti** | spaghetti |
| **Speisekarte** | menu |
| **spielen** | play |
| **Spinat** | spinach |
| **Steak** | steak |
| **Stern** | star |
| **Stiefel** | boots |
| **Straße** | street |
| **Stuhl** | chair |
| **Südafrika** | South Africa |
| **Supermarkt** | supermarket |
| **Süßwarengeschäft** | sweet shop |

### T

| | |
|---|---|
| **Tafel** | board |
| **tanzen** | dance |
| **Tasche** | bag |
| **Tasse** | cup |
| **Teddybär** | teddy bear |
| **Tee** | tea |
| **Tennis** (spielen) | (play) tennis |
| **Tier** | animal |
| **Tisch** | table |
| **Toast** | toast |
| **Tomate** | tomato |
| **Torte** | cake |
| Kleidung **tragen** | wear |

| | |
|---|---|
| **traurig** | sad |
| **Treppe(n)** | stairs |
| **trinken** | drink |
| **T-Shirt** | T-shirt |
| **Tür** | door |
| **Turnschuhe** | trainers |

### U

| | |
|---|---|
| **U-Bahn** | underground |
| Mir ist **übel.** | I feel sick. |
| **und** | and |
| **unser/e** | our |
| **unter** | under |
| **Urkunde** | certificate |

### V

| | |
|---|---|
| **verängstigt** | scared |
| **vergessen** | forget (Vergangenheit: forgot) |
| **verschneit** | snowy |
| **vervollständigen** | complete |
| **verwenden** | use |
| **viel/e** | a lot of/lots of |
| **viertel nach (neun)** | quarter past (nine) |
| **viertel vor (elf)** | quarter to (eleven) |
| **Volleyball (spielen)** | (play) volleyball |
| **von dort oben** | from up there |
| **vor** | in front of |
| **Vorhänge** | curtains |
| **vorsichtig** | careful |

### W

| | |
|---|---|
| **warm** | warm |
| **was** | what |
| **weiß** | white |
| **Wellensittich** | budgie |
| **wer** | who |
| **Wetter** | weather |
| **wie** | how |
| **wie viel** | how much |
| **wie viel/e** | how many |
| **Wien** | Vienna |
| **Wind** | wind |
| **windig** | windy |
| **Winter** | winter |
| **wir** | we |
| **wissen** | know |
| **wo** | where |
| **Wohnzimmer** | living room |
| **Wolke** | cloud |
| **Wollmütze** | woolly hat |
| **Wort** | word |
| **Würstchen** | sausages |
| **wütend** | angry |

### Z

| | |
|---|---|
| **Zahl** | number |
| **zählen** | count |
| **Zahn/Zähne** | tooth/teeth |
| **Zeh(en)** | toe(s) |
| **zeichnen** | draw |
| **Zeit** | time |
| **Zimmer** | room |
| **Zoo** | zoo |
| **zu Hause** | at home |
| **Zucker** | sugar |
| **zuordnen** | match |
| **Zwiebel** | onion |

## Zahlen

| | | | | | | | |
|---|---|---|---|---|---|---|---|
| 1 | one | 35 | thirty-five | 69 | sixty-nine |
| 2 | two | 36 | thirty-six | 70 | seventy |
| 3 | three | 37 | thirty-seven | 71 | seventy-one |
| 4 | four | 38 | thirty-eight | 72 | seventy-two |
| 5 | five | 39 | thirty-nine | 73 | seventy-three |
| 6 | six | 40 | forty | 74 | seventy-four |
| 7 | seven | 41 | forty-one | 75 | seventy-five |
| 8 | eight | 42 | forty-two | 76 | seventy-six |
| 9 | nine | 43 | forty-three | 77 | seventy-seven |
| 10 | ten | 44 | forty-four | 78 | seventy-eight |
| 11 | eleven | 45 | forty-five | 79 | seventy-nine |
| 12 | twelve | 46 | forty-six | 80 | eighty |
| 13 | thirteen | 47 | forty-seven | 81 | eighty-one |
| 14 | fourteen | 48 | forty-eight | 82 | eighty-two |
| 15 | fifteen | 49 | forty-nine | 83 | eighty-three |
| 16 | sixteen | 50 | fifty | 84 | eighty-four |
| 17 | seventeen | 51 | fifty-one | 85 | eighty-five |
| 18 | eighteen | 52 | fifty-two | 86 | eighty-six |
| 19 | nineteen | 53 | fifty-three | 87 | eighty-seven |
| 20 | twenty | 54 | fifty-four | 88 | eighty-eight |
| 21 | twenty-one | 55 | fifty-five | 89 | eighty-nine |
| 22 | twenty-two | 56 | fifty-six | 90 | ninety |
| 23 | twenty-three | 57 | fifty-seven | 91 | ninety-one |
| 24 | twenty-four | 58 | fifty-eight | 92 | ninety-two |
| 25 | twenty-five | 59 | fifty-nine | 93 | ninety-three |
| 26 | twenty-six | 60 | sixty | 94 | ninety-four |
| 27 | twenty-seven | 61 | sixty-one | 95 | ninety-five |
| 28 | twenty-eight | 62 | sixty-two | 96 | ninety-six |
| 29 | twenty-nine | 63 | sixty-three | 97 | ninety-seven |
| 30 | thirty | 64 | sixty-four | 98 | ninety-eight |
| 31 | thirty-one | 65 | sixty-five | 99 | ninety-nine |
| 32 | thirty-two | 66 | sixty-six | 100 | a hundred |
| 33 | thirty-three | 67 | sixty-seven | | |
| 34 | thirty-four | 68 | sixty-eight | | |

## Fragewörter

| | | | |
|---|---|---|---|
| **Who?** | Wer? | **Who** is your English teacher? | **Wer** ist dein/e Englischlehrer/in? |
| **Where?** | Wo? | **Where** is the supermarket? | **Wo** ist der Supermarkt? |
| **How?** | Wie? | **How** are you? | **Wie** geht es dir? |
| **How many?** | Wie viel/e? | **How many** children are in your class? | **Wie viele** Kinder sind in deiner Klasse? |
| **How much?** | Wie viel? | **How much** is the T-shirt? | **Wie viel** kostet das T-Shirt? |
| **What?** | Was? | **What** would you like to eat? | **Was** möchtest du gerne essen? |
| | | **What's for dinner?** | Was gibt es zum Abendessen? |
| | | **What's the matter/problem?** | Was ist los? |
| | | **What's missing?** | Was fehlt? |
| | | **What's your grandpa's name?** | Wie heißt dein Großvater? |
| | | **What's the time?** | Wie spät ist es? |
| | | **What's the weather like?** | Wie ist das Wetter? |

## Persönliche Fürwörter

| | | |
|---|---|---|
| **I** | ich | I **am** ten. |
| **you** | du | You **are** ten. |
| **he/she/it** | er/sie/es | He/she/it **is** eleven. |
| **we** | wir | We **are** eleven. |
| **you** | ihr | You **are** eight. |
| **they** | sie (Mehrzahl) | They **are** twelve. |

## Britische Währung

**£1** (one pound) = **100p** (a hundred pence)

PLAYWAY plus • G. Gerngross, H. Puchta, C. Becker • © 2012 HELBLING, Rum/Innsbruck